PIGGERY-JOKERY IN TONGA

In Search Of The Friendly Islands

Andrew Sparke

Piggery-Jokery In Tonga: In Search Of The Friendly Islands

APS Publications,
4 Oakleigh Road,
Stourbridge,
West Midlands,
DY8 2JX

www.andrewsparke.com

CONTENTS

THE DECISION TO GO

We arrive in Tonga, Paul and I, on a business trip which rapidly evolves into a fraud investigation and ultimately into giving evidence to a Royal Inquiry for King George Tupou V into land transactions across the islands. We come to Vava'u hoping to create employment and earn some money and on both counts we ultimately fail. But what we do get is a glimpse of a hugely attractive culture and make friends within days that I'm desperate to go back to meet again. I also accidentally while drunk nearly get married. But that comes later.

Tonga is both very foreign and very familiar. Any country that lets un-corralled pigs wander down the Main Street but has English as its primary language after Tongan and whose religious leanings are towards Methodism, Catholicism and Mormonism will seem both familiar and excitingly alien at one and the same time.

Paul has been planning to visit Tonga for ages. I occasionally act as his legal adviser but I wasn't party to the deposit he made with an American land agent. I was however booking a five week break to see friends in Australia. Before leaving I get a telephone invitation to meet Paul in Sydney and travel to Tonga with him, really as nothing more glamorous than his carer. He needs knee surgery, can hardly walk and his wife, who's tied up with her own work and can't make the trip, understandably doesn't trust him travelling on his own. He's offering to subsidise ten days of my holiday if I say yes. So I say yes. One of the better decisions in my life. And really as it turns out he needs a lawyer with him and we cram months' worth of fascinating work and experiences into the short time we're there.

Why Paul wanted a plantation is worth a book of its own. Suffice to say he'd been buggering around in Nevis for years trying to get one of his pet projects off the ground and he kept running into red tape of the governmental variety, inertia and distrust of foreigners. The project he had in mind and which he is now preparing to move lock stock and barrel to Tonga is about commercial exploitation of a plant called Jatropha.

Jatropha is an olive like plant. Its fruit is juicy but bitter. Even goats won't eat it. This means subject to decent soil, adequate water supply and a warm climate you're as near as dammit guaranteed a good crop. And the fruit when crushed yields oil you can simply burn. You can use it directly in a power plant to generate electricity or modify it with a simple chemical process to create a diesel substitute and run farm and marine engines with it. The only downside of producing fuel from Jatropha is that the refining process leaves glycerol as a waste product. And glycerol is expensive to dispose of. However if you set up a soap manufacturing entity right next door you can use the glycerol in a virtuous circle and create extra local jobs. It all sounds good especially when Paul discovers Air New Zealand are already test-flying a Boeing 747 on a fifty percent Jatropha mixture and are reporting improved fuel efficiency.

The plantation he has in mind is called Mandarin Estates on the small island of Fofoa near Vava'u, placed for sale with a gushing internet listing including the following salient details covering the plantation, the residential lot and the buildings:

... an 80 year term... the full asking price is just $145,000 US Dollars...

The land agent marketing Mandarin Estates agreed to purchase the property for Paul treating the purchase price as a loan and agreeing to convey title to Paul once the loan of the purchase price was repaid.

So the purpose of this trip is to see Fofoa, settle the transfer of the plantation from the land agent to Paul in return for the balance of the purchase price after the deduction of £10,000 in loan instalments already repaid, resolve the importation obstacles for Jatropha seed and prepare the ground for Paul and family to move to Tonga as a main base away from the UK.

What follows is a travelogue, a detective mystery, and a cultural tour of a little-known part of the world which ideally needs to be visited before it changes. And the unique cultures of this region are already threatened by Chinese investment aiming to secure mineral rights in return for services and infra-structure which until now the islands have managed quite happily without.

SO WHERE ARE WE OFF TO?

The Kingdom of Tonga comprises 171 islands, many of them uninhabited coral atolls, located in the Pacific Ocean. To put matters roughly in context The Friendly Islands can be found not far from Fiji, well to the north east of Australia, and north of New Zealand

The population of Tonga is about 100,000 concentrated in Tongatapu and the islands of 'Eua, Ha'apai and Vava'u. After Tongatapu itself Tonga's second largest town is Neiafu, situated on Vava'u. It is home to some 6,000 people and blessed with a deep-water port of some significance.

Neiafu is our planned destination.

FLYING THE BASIC WAY

The flight from Sydney to Tongatapu is civilised and uneventful. We are talking Virgin Blue here so you'd expect no different. The only problem is that it's a late evening arrival. No problem for my well organised friend who's found us lodgings and a car is waiting at the airport to pick us up. At the house where we're to stay a Tongan banquet for two is set out on the table because "You said you'd want to eat something Tongan". We also have to wolf down pieces of birthday cake saved for us from a family celebration earlier in the day. Then there's a sumptuous bed in the main house for Paul and a shack in the garden for me. I don't care much. We've got about four hours sleep till the taxi comes back for us.

Fua'amotu International looks respectably modern in the early morning light. But we're being dumped next door at the domestic airport where check-in is one desk in a small office with six or seven other people wanting to reach Vava'u.

On the apron our plane is a shiny, if aging, silver thing with a propeller on each wing. Our main bags are in the hold but hand luggage can't go in the cabin for reasons of ideal weight distribution. That all gets lodged in the aircraft's nose cone. Take my seat, pray a little and relax into the inevitability of whatever fate awaits.

We're forty to fifty minutes in the air and the view of the blue Pacific dotted with islands is truly magical. Descending over Vava'u my gaze is drawn to a white iced cake of a building in the town. Later I learn it's St Joseph's, the Catholic Cathedral.

There are no great formalities at Vava'u. We collect our bags and walk off the runway into the waiting minivan hired by our smiling land agent.

FIRST CONTACTS

James is standing beside his elderly minivan. A stocky Tongan with a perpetual smile he grabs our bags and loads them. A couple of Americans join us while others pile into a second taxi and then we're off. The land agent has already explained that the whole group will tour half a dozen properties and business opportunities rather than splitting up. First stop is coffee at the Crow's Nest Café and lunch for those who want it. That definitely includes me, having seen and smelt the massive hamburger one of the café regulars is tucking into.

We stay at the café a while so that the owner can discuss the business with a couple of the American prospects looking to buy into a venture which will enable them to re-locate to Tonga. Shamelessly earwigging, we learn quite a bit about Tonga and land deals in a few minutes. Resolve to come back and talk to Steve and his wife another day.

Moving on we look at some beautiful properties but although we tackle him about it, Paul and I can't get a firm date and time out of the land agent for us to get over to Fofoa to see Mandarin Estates. "Nobody lives there of course. We'll have to get hold of the owner. And arrange a boat…" But our visit has been arranged for weeks. Why isn't a trip across to Fofoa already a firm part of the itinerary? Our hackles are up a bit when he says that nothing can be done over the weekend but at least he undertakes to meet up on Monday and bring us the legal papers we need to have checked out before the transaction can be completed.

When the tour is done, James takes us to the house we've arranged to stay in. He drives carefully but on the main road still has to brake sharply to avoid a loose pig on the road. It seems it's worse to hit a pig here than a child. Pigs have real financial value because they're required for every Tongan celebration – wedding, funeral, whatever - roast a pig. And somebody owns every wandering, apparently wild, pig. Kill one and there's a big compensation bill. A child, on the other hand, is just a financial drain on its family until it's old enough to earn its keep.

In fact deliberately killing someone's pig is a serious insult. We were told of a family feud which escalated alarmingly after one brother killed, cooked and served up the other's dog and the dog's owner paid him back by doing the same with his pig.

BASE CAMPS

The house we've rented for the week is in the middle of a large estate of bungalows and shanties built higgledy-piggledy up the hillside from the Fatafehi Road. It's got a great view over trees and water and, if a little basic, it's still comfortable. Mind you the water supply as we discover can be a little erratic on occasion when the house cistern runs low on captured rainwater so taking a shower isn't always possible. But the main problem for Paul is that it's a bit of a pull up from the main road and then quite a walk into town. For Paul on crutches it's an impossibility. We quickly find the card James gave us and hire him on an as-and-when needed basis.

The house is also a bit remote for people to find us so we need a working base or two. I'm already planning to spend time at the Crow's Nest Café which seems to me both a mine of potential information and the purveyor of the finest hamburgers I've ever eaten. What it lacks is computer access. We need a Cyber Café to become Paul's base. James suggests an establishment on the road into town called the Aquarium Café. The view and the friendliness of Mike and Lori, the owners, seals the deal. The new Dickinson-Sparke headquarters is determined.

At the end of the day we ask James to drive us round the island to see what's here. Towards the end of the ride he takes us to the Tongan Beach Resort and that immediately gets our unanimous vote as the out-of-town office for lazy hot afternoon discussions on sun-loungers underneath the palm trees and for bathing in the sultry shallow waters beside which Dieter Dyck has chosen to set up his little holiday community.

Dieter's personal history is a story in its own right. Escaping as a young boy from the ruins of post-war Germany he ended up in New Zealand, married to a Tongan woman and with, for many years, a highly successful business. Only when that business failed did he start all over again with all the enthusiasm of a man decades younger than he was and establish his home and a holiday resort in his wife's native land. If you get the chance to stay at Tongan Beach in one of the little bungalows fronting the shore, you absolutely must. You may never want to go home again.

IN CONVERSATION WITH SALESI

Salesi Peae is a very wealthy man by Tongan standards. Indeed he is said to be either the second or third richest man in the kingdom after the King depending on whether Salesi's brother is either the third or the second richest man in Tonga. Estimates vary. He is also it seems a very kind man who wears his wealth lightly. Of course this may be in part because we caught him at the ideal moment when he was bored rigid and our project gave him something to think about. He had been very unwell and was told by doctors his condition was incurable. So he started winding up his affairs and liquidating his many business interests. Then somebody offered him an unexpected avenue of hope and he went for treatment in New Zealand and came back with a new lease of life but nothing to vent his energies on. Then we turn up.

Our only connection with Salesi at the outset is that we're renting one of his houses for our stay in Vava'u. When James delivers us to the front door, Salesi 's there in person with the keys. He turns up the next day to cut the grass and deliver a huge basket of fruit for us, stays for a drink, is openly curious about what we are doing in Tonga, somehow convincing us to trust him with the details, makes an offer of assistance and invites us to watch the rugby with him on the following Saturday.

He also makes it abundantly clear that although the house isn't in one of the most salubrious parts of the island, it's his community and people know the house is his and so everybody will help us and nobody will even entertain the thought of stealing from us even if we leave the doors wide open. He is of course right and the people around us prove amazingly friendly and equally curious.

Salesi is as good as his word, seizing on one issue he can immediately do something about. Paul had shipped a load of Jatropha seeds in and they are stuck in a customs warehouse. Salesi says he'll sort it and does. He also gives us contacts to see, allowing us to take his name in vain to get a foot in the door. The most important name he gives us is Hanateli. We'll get to him later.

It's a shame though that so far we've not been able to return to Tonga because Salesi suggests that, when we do, we bring with us the finest bottle of wine we can find and he'll introduce us to a close friend, who's really interested in alternative energy and in a position to make things happen if he likes us and our plans. This paragon just happens to loves red wine. The man he has in mind is King George.

By this time I'm really looking forward to picking Salesi's brains again but we need to see Paul's plantation first and get some ground work done.

THE DANCING ROOSTER

Work in Tonga is about as idiosyncratic as anything can be.

To start with if you have your own business and more than one employee you are tied to it. If you want it to be profitable. Even if you employ local people, you have to be there to manage in person. You can't hire somebody local, however well-educated and experienced, to supervise your employees for you. This is because beneath the surface lurks an incomprehensible mesh of subtle family status and class distinctions. And somebody of a slightly higher class can never under any circumstances submit to being supervised by a social inferior. This rather limits the scale of local enterprises unless they are run and well managed by so-called *palangi*, non-Tongans. Basically British, German, American, Australian and New Zealander ex-patriates.

That said work is done at a snail's pace over coffee and other refreshments and stress levels are low. Unless you come in from outside wanting to get something done quickly. For example asking a question about the opening hours of the bank or the Land Office will get you a pretty ambiguous answer.

The Tongan culture puts politeness, friendliness and relationships above such mundane things as making money. This is fine if you are yourself a social creature, interested in other human beings and possess lashings of patience. As someone who knows from Day One that my role will be to make all the contacts Paul can exploit whilst he will install himself on his crutches for much of the time in the cyber café, asking those he needs to see, such as our American land agent, to meet him there. While he polishes a chair with his arse and uses his brain I will need to be ducking and diving around the town of Neiafu, starting every morning with breakfast at the Crow's Nest Café, close to the docks, a haunt of European business people and engineers off the various ships coming in and out of port.

The owners of The Crow's Nest are an energetic couple called Steve and Tess, hailing respectively from Australia and New Zealand. This was their new start in the catering trade and they seem to know everybody and everything that's happening on the island. They are also engaged in marketing their business through our land agent because the dream move they're hoping to make next is to Chile. In consequence they know all the problems surrounding buying land in Tonga and since Paul and I aren't in the market to buy a café, they feel free to be brutally frank about things. And they introduce me to people who know even more. Starting with a leading question. "Do you play darts?"

I can play a bit but only because of misspent teenage years in the pub of a Devonshire seaside town which virtually closed down in winter. I say so.

"Then come and join us down the Dancing Rooster tonight. James will know where it is." Steve is already aware we've got the minibus driver on a retainer to ferry us around. You can't keep much secret in a place the size of Neiafu.

So as we eat breakfast and swill coffee, we discuss tennis, Steve's preferred sport, the music we like and a *fakaleiti* show Steve and Tess had been to the night before. *Fakaleiti* are boys dressed and raised from birth as girls, frequently in households where there are a preponderance of male children and someone needs to be conditioned to perform the household and caring roles for aging parents. And in between such weighty and fascinating subjects I learn something about land title and transactions in Tonga. Already what I can scent, ignoring the distraction of Steve's freshly baked bread rolls, has more than a hint of a scam about it but of course Paul and I have to prove it. And we have mere days to do just that. Next stop for me is going to be the Land Office for some in-depth trawling through legal papers, something I've largely ducked out of doing since qualifying as a solicitor. But there's no clerk to help this time so needs must. Time to get my fingers dusty.

Except that I don't have the lot numbers and the island of Fofoa contains a good many more acres than the plot Paul's interested in. And anyway the Land Office is shut over the weekend and possibly on Monday too. So back to confer with Paul at the Aquarium Café where he's already set up his mobile office and is open for business with the UK and the rest of the world. He doesn't seem too concerned about visiting a bar on his crutches later so The Dancing Rooster it is definitely going to be.

Just a warning for anybody about to visit the bar at the Dancing Rooster for the first time. The stairs down to the bar are crazily steep and slippery. Paul, unstable on his pins and using his crutches, traverses most of them on the way in, while stone-cold sober, on his arse having fallen at the first. He insists his health warning goes into this book.

It seems that after coffee, more business gets done in bars In Tonga than anywhere else so we feel right at home in the Dancing Rooster. The restaurant, the main end of Gunther the owner and chef's business, looks desperately empty early evening whereas the small alcohol servery down in the basement is heaving. No Tongans at all. They have homes to go to. Gunther's trade in beer and spirits is all ex-pat. Mainly Brits and Germans. Have a long conversation with a boozed-up

German who's out-stayed his visa by ten years and can't work out how to get home for a relative's funeral. Or more precisely, if he leaves Tonga, how to get back in.

Then Steve turns up with a local businessman who obviously originated from Essex and who wants to talk non-stop through several darts matches. And he keeps buying drinks. Nice fellow. At some point Steve mentions our interest in land agents and Paul, by now safely lodged on a stool with his crutches in the corner out the way, and I listen avidly to an outpouring of what we need to know, hardly having to do more than prompt with an occasional question. Leads for us to check out and names flood out. Names which will become intensely familiar to us in the days to come. Bryce, Jefferson, Schmeiser...they're all there in the Royal Inquiry report at the back of this book if you want to know more about them.

We get home somehow. I think James comes and collects us. Paul recollects differently claiming he's so drunk he insists we walk home, crutches and all. Perhaps we do, with, in his case, alcohol acting as a superior painkiller. What I do remember is somebody insisting as we leave that I come and play at the Tennis Club. Me who couldn't hit a tennis ball if they let me play with a double-size racquet!

EXPLORATION

Before further considering the human inhabitants of the islands, it might be worth touching on the animal and insect life. We see some truly impressive spiders out and about but if you discount mosquito bites, the only really aggressive species we come across is a massive centipede Paul finds in his bed one night. Confronted by my friend, it rears up and tries to bite him. When he swats it onto the floor, it scuttles away and his ongoing relief not to see it again remains one of his abiding recollections of the trip. Later the pharmacist's wife, another

Kiwi, tells him her husband has been so badly bitten by a large centipede that he's had to go off-island for treatment.

Waking up good and early is facilitated by another native denizen: the fruit-bat. Great colonies of them settle in the trees during the warmth of the day and come to life extremely noisily at sundown. A second spate of activity disturbs the middle of the night as they return to feed their young and then there's the dawn chorus to tell the world they're settling down for a few hours.

Turning to homo sapiens, Neiafu has a population of a little over 6000 people. There are a few hundred more in the town's vicinity of which about 250 or so are white immigrants. There is in addition a growing Chinese presence.

It's explained to me that the ethnically white inhabitants came in three waves. The early arrivals in search of paradise married Tongans and disappeared into subsistence farming as a way of life. The second wave in the 1970s and 1980s came with better thought -out plans to make a living but still ended up in one-man businesses adding little to the local economy. The third wave of perhaps 100 to 150 individuals came to establish businesses which would bring new jobs for local people whilst providing a high standard of living and quality of life for the immigrants themselves. Most of the whites visible in Neiafu are from the third wave and whether British or German or Aussie or Kiwi or American they know each other well and rapidly pull in any new arrivals of interest like Paul and me. No secrets here!

And everybody we speak to seems very wary of land agents including ours. He does at least turn up late in the day on Monday to a meeting at the Aquarium. Fortuitously as it turns out he comes at the same time as Salesi who we've invited for coffee and a chat. It's watching the land agent's glib responses to Salesi's pointed questions which escalates my concerns. Still no visit is on the cards to Fofoa and he's brought no documents with him. Exasperated, Paul insists that he provide lot numbers, copy title deeds and a copy of his contract with the vendor which he agrees to do. Despite email reminders of the urgency of the matter in the following days, he doesn't.

We aren't at all sure what to do in the face of the land agent's inaction. The one thing that seems sensible is to talk to the others who came in on the same flight as us to do deals with our land agent. We share our concerns with three Americans. A couple who want to relocate on the husband's retirement from the US military and a former ballet dancer called Shannon who's here as the advance guard on behalf of her husband, parents and daughters to find a new home and business opportunity to take them away from what she describes as an increasingly hectic and unsustainable lifestyle in New York.

They are all a little disillusioned already but not for the same reasons as us. Shannon can't see how to make enough income in Tonga and Is concerned about the available medical care as her parents get older. The army officer really likes Tonga but his wife, a true and lovely Southern belle, feels things are all too basic for her to enjoy living in Tonga. She's probably right and they are flying home earlier than the rest of us anyway. Still we agree to share notes and findings with Shannon and we now have some company for broader explorations of the island.

We go to remote beaches to swim, return time and again to Dieter's resort, arrange to see Hanoteli's very special gardens at Ene'io and to take Shannon with us to the rugby. The promised trip over to Fofoa to see the Mandarin Estates still doesn't materialise.

There isn't that much in the shops before the tourist season proper starts in May but I do buy something for myself I still treasure. A genuine Tongan dirt shirt. It's a polo shirt, well made and then dyed with the island's rich red clay. It comes out a bright orange colour and you have the choice whether to wash it in cold salt water to fix the dye or allow the sun to get at it and have it fade naturally in the elements. I let mine fade and six years later I'm still wearing it and it's as comfortable as an old friend. I can't get another one from Treasure Trove in Neiafu without going back there. I've tried but they've no reliable way of mailing them. So if anybody's going to Vava'u I'd pay over the odds to have another one brought back.

Shannon and I also tour the markets which yield up interesting fruit and vegetables. Paul benefits because I take to cooking in the evenings, adding cheese or meat from the little grocery on the estate to whatever we've haggled over with the stall holders or the Chinese provisions merchant James takes me to.

From our visits to the markets and cafes frequented by Tongans rather than palangi, we discover that when it comes to food, there are fascinating differences between us. To start with Tongans have an amazingly sweet tooth. They shovel copious quantities of sugar into their coffee and Tongan mothers commonly put drinks such as Coca Cola, Sprite and Fanta into their infants' bottles. A favourite Tongan snack is to take a loaf of the local bread, tear off one end, pour in a can of coke and then eat it.

Palangi are not allowed to bake and sell white bread. This is reserved for locals. Their bread is a little sweet for European tastes. Commercial palangi bakers get round this by adding whole-meal or anything else that comes to hand to their bread thus making it an odd light brown colour but also much more healthy and substantial. Wonderful stuff and edible for days even without butter.

Finally Tongans think palangi are mad for keeping pets they don't intend to eat.

Shannon and I also find out, in an alarming situation, to trust the native courtesy and friendliness of Tongans. We've been enjoying Gunther's famous lobster dish and sit in his restaurant until the early hours of the morning putting the world to rights. Coming out of The Dancing rooster, Shannon's guest house is in the opposite direction to the house Paul's rented but being English and reasonably well dragged-up, I insist, against her protests that it's unnecessary, on walking her safely home. It's a lovely warm night for a walk anyway. As we come down a slight hill our way is blocked by three big Tongan lads very much the worse for drink. I whisper to Shannon that at the first sign of trouble I'm pushing the one on the left over and she's to make a run for it through the gap. My heroic thought is completely redundant. In very slurred tones, the lads stop to ask if we've had a great night and wish us all the best for tomorrow. I can't help thinking the end result of a similar situation in Britain might be very different.

THE RUGBY

Saturday dawns and as instructed we're up early. Shannon's taxi arrives and drops her off at our house and a few minutes later Salesi's here in his big four by four, a clutch of scaffolding poles for one of his building sites racked up on the back. And our education in the Tongan approach to rugby begins.

The ground is pretty large and there's a good crowd already. Although there are no grandstands. No seating of any kind. Play's already underway to my surprise. But then I hadn't realised we'd be here all day with matches featuring all the local sides from miles around playing consecutively in back to back games. Tongan linesmen and umpires obviously need to be extremely fit themselves.

In fact so keen is everyone to play on Saturday that those from the outlying islands have sailed in at dawn to get some team practice before the matches proper kick off. Salesi's local team apparently gathered a day or two before and camped behind his house to do their training. You'll gather this is sport taken very seriously indeed.

Salesi drives in, one of a procession of cars jockeying into the ground, circles the perimeter of the pitch and parks on the far side, just short of the half way line. We all get out; greet the linesman running past our noses and sit cross-legged on the grass. It's all a bit different to watching Stourbridge Town trying to out-pass their opponents back in the Midlands.

The way they play is different too. There's a frightening level of physical commitment as they charge the ball down. Nobody pulls out of any tackle and it's a wonder that there aren't casualties galore in every match. But there aren't. These are hardened young men in their prime. We take the mickey out of Shannon and her devotion to American Football. "Now this is a real mans' game!" Then Salesi placates her by telling us that his son played rugby but has had to bulk up to take advantage of a scholarship offer to play football for an American university and he affirms that that too is a pretty tough game although many of the injuries come from helmet impact which isn't an issue in rugby.

The day gets hotter. No food is available and despite a decent breakfast of rolls, cheese, meat and fruit before leaving home, I'm getting hungry. And thirsty. No beer though. No cans of fizzy pop. A man with a portable icebox takes a few pa'angas off me and gives me the only thing he has to sell. A green coconut with a hole drilled in it so you can swig the fluid inside. And it is refreshing and entirely climate-appropriate. Find myself enjoying it and having another one later.

Eventually we've all had enough and hop back in the four by four. Salesi takes the short cut over the edge of the bank and with a rattling crash, the scaffolding poles go off the back. Salesi's in the driving seat, Paul's on crutches and Shannon's a petite ex-ballet dancer. I on the other hand am six foot two, slightly overweight but strong and with no obvious excuses. I give in to the inevitable and leaping out, start wedging the steel poles back on the four by four, And a loud voice shouts out in a strong English accent "Bloody hell! Might have known it was you, Sparke!" Look up, knowing that I've already found a place for myself in Vava'u because the grinning man behind the wheel of the VW van held up behind Salesi is my darts partner from the other night in the bar. Lance. Formerly from Essex in case you couldn't tell - to quote Ian Dury.

Of course we end up back at The Dancing Rooster. It's another late night.

A RIVAL FOR KEW GARDENS

Haniteli Fa'anunu and his wife Lucy have a continuing dream. Inspired by Kew Gardens in England, he wants to create a Polynesian rival on a grand scale. The result is the ever-growing Ene'io Botanical Garden near Neiafu which has the largest and most varied plant collection, not only in in the Kingdom of Tonga but in that vast area of the southern hemisphere. It consists of 22 acres, is in private ownership and Hanateli offers visitors a personalized tour with his own enthusiastic commentary. The garden reputedly contains over 100 plant families and 500 plant species, both native and exotic and has one thing Kew can never match, a private beach and camping area. He and his wife also cook a mean fish dish if you choose to eat at Ene'io.

We get the tour of the garden by jeep. It's terminated early because we're all being bitten to death by mosquitos. The compensation is a cracking lunch washed down with more coconut milk but the real value is the long discussion with Hanateli about Paul's intentions. Immediately Hanateli shocks us. "We already grow Jatropha here. We call it Tongan Fig"

It seems the height to which Jatropha grows makes it an ideal symbiotic plant for one of Tonga's cash crops. Jatropha's leaves provide wonderful shade for vanilla as it matures and the reason nobody realised it's the very plant we want to import is because the farmers cut off the fruiting parts so nobody has ever seen the olive-like fruit we've been showing them in photos.

This is amazing news because it proves Jatropha will flourish in the rich Tongan soils; co-cropping with vanilla increases the economic yield of any land dedicated to growing it; and, best of all, the awkward customs officers in import control can get stuffed. We don't need to import seeds at all.

Guess where we'll be going to celebrate tonight.

WHALES, SHARKS AND YACHTS

I can't claim that Vava'u is all work. We spend a lot of time in cafes and at the Tongan Beach Resort. We also meet lots of people including three hard-sunbathing young doctors-to-be from Nottingham on their so-called elective time out as medical students working in the local hospital. They're having a good break but are worried about swimming for fear of sharks. There are sharks of course but they don't come into three feet of water and it's very seldom that anybody dies from a shark-bite. I was told that the last casualty in Neiafu was some years previously when a young Peace Corps volunteer who practised deep water swimming across the sound every day, refused to heed the warnings not to do it on this particular day because the whale-watching boats had gone out churning up the water in the wake of incoming fishing boats and there was bound to be chum, fish guts and the like out in the channel.

We were unfortunately out in Tonga about a month too early for the whales. Great hump-backed whales whose breaching adds a real boost to tourism in the second half of May and through June in the region. That's partly why the big yachts come here. The first to arrive from Australia and New Zealand and then later the Americans and of course the cruise ships. And all the new shops along the waterfront open to do a roaring trade and everyone goes home thinking about investing in Tonga but most don't get round to it.

I tell the medical students that they'll be more likely to be bitten by a pig than a shark. Did you know pigs can swim? Dieter didn't. He was going mad about the occasional pig getting through the gated fence around his Tongan Beach Resort and then one morning, having his constitutional bathe, he was overtaken by a pig. It was swimming faster than he could.

CLANDESTINE MEETINGS

The land agent finally arrives at the Aquarium Café at lunchtime on Friday with a copy of the lot numbers and a plan and a copy of the contract which he states is with all the various vendors. It seems to me that he's come as late in the week as that to avoid any prospect that we can check the validity of the documents with the Land Office before I have to fly home. What he doesn't know is that I've been into the office and know they'll stay open in the afternoon for us by prior arrangement.

Before we get James to drive us to the Land Office for two o'clock when they've agreed to re-open, we go through the documents with the land agent and the figures simply don't tally. The land agent then brazenly admits that he's paid between $75,000 and $100,000 to the landowner. Nothing like the $145,000 he'd charged Paul in the loan agreement. He stands to make a personal profit of between $45,000 and $70,000 on the deal.

This is double-dealing on a breath-taking scale and if he has no valid title to pass on as we now suspect, let alone the ability to transfer an 80-year lease (something we now know to be unlawful in Tonga where the maximum lease is 20 years with an option for a further ten years) then we are talking bare-faced fraud.

We get in the minivan and James drives us straight into town. It takes no time at all to discover that the purported titles and transfers aren't registered and to discover the name of the actual registered land-owners.

That should be enough but we also manage, with some help, to track down one of the signatories to the Lease Surrender document. He's not at home but his wife shows us his passport to prove that her husband has made no agreement with our land agent and that the signature on the photocopied document is neither his nor remotely similar.

Before returning home to England, we have a party with Salesi and other friends. It turns out that Salesi owns or has a share in the restaurant. The service is great and the drinks flow. And at some point a lovely young waitress named Aia asks me in broken English if I'm single and if I would consider marrying her. Or if not, do I have any friends back home who might want a young bride. It seems she's a single mother who desperately wants a future away from Tonga. I feel sorry for her but at that point despite all the alcohol consumed, or perhaps because of it, as the old tabloid reporters used to say, I make my excuses and leave. Or I think I do. I look but she isn't at the airport when I get on the plane so I think I'm safe.

AFTERMATH

We've not been home long when we discover that a Royal Commission has been set up to look into land dealings of the sort Paul had become embroiled in and he's now invited to give evidence in writing. This we're pleased to draft and send off. It appears we have been partly instrumental in uncovering a raft of shady dealings and it's a pleasure in due course to see the matters we had run into being expertly understood and recorded for the Tongan government. Maybe the way forward for future foreign investors will be easier in consequence. Or at least with sight of the report copied below they'll know in advance what they're dealing with, as Paul patently did not when he embarked on his Jatropha project. (For the specific references to Paul's evidence see Chapter 5 of the report Sections 5.5-5.7)

And then there's the matter of the land agent we were dealing with, who's no longer living in Tonga where he allegedly faces criminal charges. Reports give his location as Nova Scotia and naturally Canada has no extradition treaty with Tonga. Paul does not of course have any of his deposit returned but then he doesn't really expect to, despite email correspondence from the man offering partial restitution. The ex-land agent in question does however host a website about how badly he has himself been ripped off in Tonga. Go to www.tongascams.com and make your own mind up.

After visiting Tonga Paul doesn't want to just abandon the project even though getting enough security over a landholding to justify capital investment seems impossible. What we have learned and now have the contacts to pursue is that he can simply deal directly with local farmers and have them gather Jatropha fruit for us from their existing shade plants. We even have a contact (oddly enough from the tennis club) to recruit farmers from his village and oversee matters. It doesn't work because as Steve told us right at the beginning "You have to be here to manage people yourself." And we aren't. Our lives are elsewhere. Shame though. Great idea and fantastic place.

Oddly a subsequent Tongan Government Energy Sustainability report doesn't even mention Jatropha which as we eventually discovered from Hanateli is already growing all over the place. In fact discriminatory international pricing has since crushed the economic viability of Tongan vanilla and on the abandoned plantations Jatropha is flourishing like topsy.

As for the title of this book that comes from one of those moments when the brain, released from its normal shackles by a pint or two of beer, does something creative without rational fore-thought. "It's been a load of jiggery-pokery hasn't it?" says Paul. "More like piggery-jokery" says I. And it stuck.

FURTHER READING

Kate ASLESON: *Tonga: Discover The Real Tonga* (2011 Other Places Publishing)
Mary M McCOY and Siotame Drew HAVEA: Making Sense Of Tonga (2006 Training Group Of The Pacific)
Jason's Kingdom Of Tonga Visitor Guide (www.jasons.com)

THE ROYAL INQUIRY

ROYAL LAND COMMISSION - SECOND INTERIM REPORT
LAND DEALINGS IN VAVA'U AND ELSEWHERE IN TONGA THROUGH THE INTERNET
MEMBERS:
BARON FIELAKEPA GCQS Chairman
LORD TUPOU KC KGCQS Commissioner
KAHUNGUNU BARRON-AFEAKI SC CRH Commissioner
GLORIA GUTTENBEIL-POLE'O MRH Secretary

EXECUTIVE SUMMARY

1. Vava'u holds immense appeal for tourists with its hilly countryside and scattered small sandy beach islands, whale watching and game fishing activities.

2. Vava'u also has great attraction for foreign investors who see the potential in attaining land with sandy beaches, developing the same and selling them to keen foreign buyers who may wish to re-locate from their country to what they see as their 'dream tropical home' away from home. Some foreigners are attracted to these lands for their own personal use in retirement and to set up their own tourist related business.

3. Early this century, a new breed of occupation began in Vava'u. These were Real Estate Agents and Commission Agents introduced by foreigners who advertised various sites and plots of land for sale through the internet. Invariably, these sites were adjoining attractive sandy beaches. On flying into Vava'u one can get a good view of the many scattered islands with beautiful sandy beaches. These are what are being marketed through the internet with the willing approval of the Tongan landowner.

4. The foreign Real Estate Agents and Commission Agents became aware that under Tongan law, there was no freehold land as they may have in their own country and the sale of land was forbidden and unlawful in Tonga. With the help of Tongan lawyers, these Agents introduced a Tenancy Agreement between the foreign buyer and the Tongan landowner under which the buyer agrees to construct buildings on the plot of land which after construction are owned by the Tongan land owner. The buildings are then rented to the foreign buyer for lengthy terms of between 50 and 99 years with an option to renew. There is an initial substantial upfront payment under the Tenancy Agreement to the Tongan landowner including the commission for the Real Estate and Commission Agents plus a smaller monthly rent payable to the Tongan landowner for the duration of the tenancy.

5. As these Tenancy Agreements involved only the occupation of a building owned by the Tongan landowner who currently retains the ownership of the land upon which the buildings rests, it is argued that this is purely a commercial contract of tenancy which is outside the strict requirements of Tongan land law, with regard to the duration of occupancy of land and the way under which land can be occupied or alienated under the provisions of the Land Act. A contrary legal opinion states that what is attempted under these Tenancy Agreements is to circumvent the principles of Tongan land law. This is unlawful under section 13 of the Land Act which provides that any dealings with regard to land that are made outside the provisions in the Act are unlawful unless approved in writing by the Minister of Lands and furthermore is punishable with a fine or imprisonment. The contrary legal opinions can only be resolved by a decision of the Court but no one has taken the matter to the court yet. The alternative is for the Legislative Assembly to legislate to clarify the position relating to such tenancy agreements.

6. There are only a handful of agents advertising land through the internet in Vava'u. The first who began this work was a Mr. Robert Bryce in 2004/2005. He has now re-located his business since 2008 to Fiji. The other main people practicing this trade in Vava'u are Mr. Nesha Rosic, Mr. Gordon Allison, Mr. Hans Schmeiser and Mr. Trevor Jefferson.

7. As might be expected with the little land available for this kind of business, there was great rivalry between these agents where Bryce worked together with Schmeiser and sometimes Jefferson while Rosic worked together with Allison. Various derogatory and defamatory remarks were published through various websites on the internet to dissuade investors from dealing with a particular agent. Some samples were tendered as Exhibits and will form part of this report.

8. In most cases, a Tongan landowner would approach one of these agents offering his land for money. The agent would bring his Tenancy Agreement to the Tongan landowner, have it explained by a Tongan and finally by a Tongan lawyer, agree to the terms and sign. At this stage the Tongan landowner would be made aware of the agreed amount that he would be getting in American currency and any amount over and above this would be for the commission and expenses of the agent. Samples of these Tenancy Agreements were also tendered as Exhibits and will form part of this report.

9. The site would then be advertised on the internet through websites of the agent. Once an interested party is found, the terms are discussed through email and eventually the Tenancy Agreement is sent to the investor for signature. Under the Tenancy Agreement a substantial payment in US dollars is to be made to the bank account of the agent or to an escrow account designated by the agent to be followed by a smaller monthly payment for rent to the bank account of the Tongan landowner. The Tenancy Agreement is between the Tongan

landowner and the foreign buyer who have often neither communicated nor met each other.

10. A form of Lease Agreement was also used by some Real Estate Agents as opposed to the Tenancy Agreement in which not only the buildings would be rented but also the land itself. These lease Agreements were for periods of up to 50 years with an option to renew 4 for periods of up to another 49 years and referred to as "family agreements" by one Real Estate Agent. After these Agreements were signed by the buyer, the parties then proceed to sign an application to lease using form L.9 of the Ministry of Lands for the legal term of 20 years, if the land is part of a tax allotment. The buyer is led to believe by the Real Estate Agent and some Tongan lawyers that the Lease Agreement is valid and binding on the Tongan landowner and his successors so the term of up to 99 years remain valid. Such agreements are unlawful under the Land Act. Sample of these Lease Agreements were tendered as Exhibit and will form part of this report.

11. This kind of land dealing was brought to the attention of Government in 2007. In 2006 Tenancy Agreements over two beach front 2 acre lots of land were entered into by a British and an American national both residing in Hong Kong with the Tongan registered land owner in the island of Nuapapu. Substantial up front money was paid to the landowner and the agent including advance payments in respect of the monthly rent. In 2007 the same land that was subject to the Tenancy Agreements was included in another Lease Agreement made by a different agent with the Tongan landowner and advertised and sold to another party and substantial payments were made to the Tongan landowner. The second Lease Agreement was negotiated by the agent on behalf of the registered landowner. A few months later the son of the landowner signed an L.9 Form application to lease for 20 years as the landowner while his father, who held the registered

title, was still alive but died 4 months later. The name of the son was entered in the Land Registration book in Vava'u with the approval of the Acting Governor on the same day as the L.9 application. The application for lease was approved by the Acting Governor of Vava'u and subsequently by Cabinet and registered. The son resides in American Samoa and could not be called to give evidence. Buildings have been constructed and advertised through the internet and already sold as villas to foreigners in pursuance of the 20 years registered lease and the 99 years family Lease Agreement.

12. The problem raised in the preceding paragraph was brought to the notice of Mr. Kahungunu Barron-Afeaki in 2007 by the parties residing in Hong Kong who had the prior Tenancy Agreements in 2006. They retained him as their lawyer. With the agreement of his clients, Mr. Afeaki sought the approval of Government in November 2007 to conduct an investigation in Vava'u with the help of the Ministry of Lands. He did this and provided a report in December 2007 which was given to Government and to his clients. The report was tendered as Exhibit 24.

13. Smaller instances of land dealings through the internet by agents were made with land in Ha'apai and Tongatapu but to a much lesser extent than at Vava'u. Reference will be made to these in the report.

14. Evidence was also given that Government through the Ministry of Labour, Commerce and Industries had put a moratorium on the issuance of Real Estate Licences as from March 2007. This moratorium was communicated verbally to the Officer in Charge in Vava'u in 2007 and she has not issued any Real Estate Licence since that date. In spite of this, Real Estate Agents have continued practicing their trade in Vava'u with impunity.

15. There were allegations of corruption by certain Government officials in relation to land dealings and this report will cover that aspect. At the outset it must be stated that many of these allegations were published through unreliable websites that lack credibility but must be mentioned here. A sample of such a website is shown in Exhibits 127, 128 and 129.

16. There were also allegations of unreliable advice given by agents, Ministry of Lands' officials, lawyers including possible conflict of interests and unprofessional conduct and these will also be covered in this report. This was given in evidence by witnesses and documents produced as exhibits in the hearing.

CHAPTER 1 – INTRODUCTION

1.1 This Interim Report covers the Second Phase of the work of the Royal Land Commission ("the Commission"). It involves an inquiry into possible unlawful sale and leases of land in Vava'u through the internet contrary to the Act of Constitution and the Land Act. Public notices of the inquiry were made in local newspapers, radio and television. Notice was also published on the website www.matangitonga.to.

1.2 Members of the public were invited to send written submissions. We received written submissions from people residing overseas and in Tonga. Some came from overseas and gave evidence at the hearings. All written submissions were considered together with the oral evidence.

Terms of Reference

1.3 The Commission's Terms of Reference required it "to inquire into all matters whatsoever concerning the land laws and practices of our Kingdom with a view to providing more effective and efficient practices." The present inquiry involves both laws and practices in Tonga over land.

Public Hearings

1.4 The hearings were open to the public and were held in the Supreme Court in Neiafu, Vava'u. In his opening statement the Chairman made it clear that the Commission were not a court of law. The Commission was to make inquiries into land practices conducted through the internet and report to His Majesty and Privy Council as required by our Terms of Appointment. The Commission cannot make decisions or solve individual problem, these would need to go through the normal processes in a court of law.

1.5 The Vava'u hearings were held on the 1st to 5th February 2010, 1st 2nd, 3rd, 9th,10th, 11th, 12th, 13th, 15th, 16th, 17th, 18th, 19th, March 2010. A total of 18 days.

1.6 Because some witnesses were in Tongatapu the Commission held hearings in the Commission's Conference Room on the 23rd, 24th, 26th, February 2010 and 16th, April 2010. A total of 4 days.

1.7 The final public hearings were held at the Conference Room of the Janful International Dateline Hotel, Nuku'alofa on the 22nd, 23rd, 27th, 28th, 29th, 30th, April 2010. A total of 6 days.

Witnesses

1.8 The Commission summonsed witnesses and heard their evidence under oath. There were a total of 57 witnesses summonsed and some had to be re-called to give further evidence. The names of witnesses (in alphabetical order) who appeared and their days of appearances are listed in the Schedule below.

1.9 Some witnesses were overseas and could not be heard in person. Written questions were made to these witnesses and answers were given. These will be included as part of the Appendices.

Schedule – Witnesses Summonsed

1. 'AKOLO, HON. LISIATE (Minister of Labour, Commerce & Industries) Tongatapu Friday, 16 April 2010
2. ALLISON, GORDON (Foreign Investor & Owner of Escape Vava'u Ltd) Vava'u Tuesday, 02 March 2010, Wednesday, 03 March 2010, Friday, 12 March 2010
3. ARNOTT, 'OFA Vava'u Monday, 15 March 2010
4. BING, ROSAMOND (Law Practitioner) Tongatapu Wednesday, 28 April 2010
5. BURGOON, PAUL (Business owner) Vava'u Tuesday, 16 March 2010
6. CORBETT, DAVID (Law Practitioner) Tongatapu Tuesday, 27 April 2010, Friday, 30 April 2010
7. FALETAU, TANIELA (Deputy Police Commander, Ministry of Police) Tongatapu Friday, 23 April 2010
8. FAU, PAULA PAU'U (ex employee of Hasdra Real Estate) Tongatapu Thursday, 22 April 201010
9. FA'APOI, HASTING (owner of Hadra Real Estate & Capital Realty) Tongatapu Tuesday, 27 April 2010, Friday, 30 April 2010
10. FA'OLIU, RINGO (Officer-in-Charge of Building Control Division, Ministry of Works) Tongatapu Tuesday, 27 April 2010, Friday, 30 April 2010
11. FE'AOMOEATA, HEILALA Tongatapu Thursday, 22 April 2010
12. FIFITA, FELISIANO TOLATI (Land Owner) Tongatapu Wednesday, 24 February 2010

13. FOTU, SALESI (Deputy Secretary, Ministry of Lands, Survey & Natural Resources) Tongatapu Friday, 23 April 2010, Friday, 30 April 2010

14. FUNAKI, HON. FINEASI (Minister of Tourism) Tongatapu Friday, 16 April 2010

15. FUSIMALOHI, VIKA (ex Deputy Secretary of the Ministry of Labour, Commerce & Industries) Tongatapu Friday, 23 April 2010

16. HALAHINGANO, PEAU Vava'u Saturday, 13 March 2010

17. HALATANU, FATAUA (Land Registration Officer, Ministry of Lands, Survey & Natural Resources) Tongatapu Tuesday, 02 February 2010 Tuesday, 23 February 2010

18. HALATUITUIA, DR NAILASIKAU (CEO - Ministry of Lands, Survey & Natural Resources) Tongatapu Friday, 26 February 2010

19. HALA'API'API, PITA VI (Land Developer – Vava'u) Vava'u Tuesday, 16 March 2010, Friday, 19 March 2010

20. HANSEN, SINALI Vava'u Friday, 05 February 2010

21. HEMALOTO, SAILOSI (Land owner – Vava'u) Vava'u Tuesday, 16 March 2010

22. JAMES, TERESA (Owner of Reef Resort, 'Otea, Vava'u) UK/Vava'u Monday, 15 March 2010

23. JEFFERSON, TREVOR (Land Agent – Vava'u) Vava'u Thursday, 18 March 2010

24. KAVA, VAO'ESE (Land Agent – Tongatapu – Market Tonga) Tongatapu Thursday, 22 April 2010, Wednesday, 28 April 2010

25. KELLEY, ALEXANDER CHRISTOPHER (Police Commander, Ministry of Police) Tongatapu Friday, 23 April 2010

26. KIVALU, SATEKI (Town officer – Nuapapu, Vava'u) Vava'u Friday, 12 March 201011

27. LATU, FOLOKE (ANZ Employee, Vava'u Branch) Vava'u Friday, 19 March 2010

28. LAVAKEI'AHO, PENI (Building Control Division, Ministry of Works) Tongatapu Friday, 30 March 2010

29. LO'AMANU, PAULA MOA (Surveyor, Ministry of Lands, Survey & Natural Resources, Vava'u) Vava'u Friday, 12 March 2010

30. MAFI, MAKAFILIA (ex Land Registration Officer, Ministry of Lands, Survey & Natural Resources, Vava'u) Vava'u Wednesday, 03 February 2010, Thursday, 04 February 2010, Saturday, 13 March 2010

31. MOALA, SEMISI (Land Registration Officer, Ministry of Lands, Survey & Natural Resources Tongatapu Friday, 23 April 2010

32. MOEAKI, TATAFU (Secretary, Ministry of Labour, Commerce & Industries) Tongatapu Friday, 16 April 2010

33. MORTIMER, RICHARD (Land investor – Nuapapu, Vava'u) Hong Kong Monday, 01 February 2010, Wednesday, 03 February 2010

34. NIU, LAKI (Law Practitioner) Tongatapu Thursday, 29 April 2010

35. PAEA, YVETTE (Branch Manager, ANZ Bank, Vava'u Branch) Vava'u Monday, 01 March 2010

36. PALU, MONALISA (Mana'ia Real Estate) Tongatapu Thursday, 22 April 2010, Friday, 23 April 2010

37. PIUKALA, KELEPI (Law Practitioner) Tongatapu Friday, 30 April 2010

38. ROSIC, NESHA (Land Agent – Vava'u – Island Real Esatet Ltd) Vava'u Tuesday, 09 March 2010, Wednesday, 10 March 2010, Friday, 19 March 2010

39. SCHMEISER, HANS (Land Agent) Vava'u Thursday, 04 February 2010 Friday, 05 February 2010, Monday, 01 March 2010, Wednesday, 17 March 2010

40. SCHMEISER, MELE Vava'u Wednesday, 17 March 2010

41. STARK, ERIC (Land investor – Nuapapu, Vava'u) Hong Kong Tuesday, 02 February 2010

42. SPROULE, DENNIS (Land investor – Nuapapu, Vava'u) Australia Tuesday, 09 March 2010

43. STEPHENSON, DANA (Law Practitioner) Tongatapu Friday, 26 February 2010, Tuesday, 27 April 2010

44. TANGI, SEFITA (Commissioner of Revenues) Tongatapu Tuesday, 23 February 2010
45. TAUFATEAU, SIONE TO'IMOANA (Law Practitioner) Vava'u Wednesday, 17 March 2010, Thursday, 18 March 2010
46. TOKE, BRUNO (Officer-in Charge, Ministry of Tourism, Vava'u) Vava'u Wednesday, 03 February 2010, Monday, 01 March 2010
47. TOKE, SAPATE (Officer-in-Charge, Ministry of Labour, Commerce & Industries, Vava'u) Vava'u Thursday, 11 March 2010
48. TONGA, CIP SISI (Officer-in-Charge, Ministry of Police, Vava'u) Vava'u Thursday, 11 March 2010, Monday, 15 March 2010
49. TU'IPULOTU, MANU Vava'u Wednesday, 03 February 2010
50. TU'ITUPOU, MASINA (Secretary, Governor's Office, Vava'u) Vava'u Thursday, 11 March 2010
51. 'UTA'ATU, CHRISTINE MARIE (Land Agent – Tongatapu – Pacific Property Development Ltd) Tongatapu Thursday, 22 April 2010
52. VAEA, SIONE MAHE (Land owner – Tu'anuku, Vava'u) Vava'u Thursday, 04 February 2010
53. VAHA'I, 'IOANE (Land owner – Tu'anuku, Vava'u) Vava'u Monday, 15 March 2010, Tuesday, 16 March 2010
54. VAILANU, SIONE (Deputy Secretary, Ministry of Labour, Commerce & Industries) Tongatapu Thursday, 22 April 2010, Tuesday, 27 April 2010
55. VAILEA, LATA Tongatapu Thursday, 22 April 2010
56. VAILEA, SANITU (Land owner – 'Otea, Vava'u) Tongatapu Friday, 23 April 2010
57. VAIPULU, HON. SAMIU (Law Practitioner & Minister of Justice) Tongatapu Thursday, 29 April 2010

Transcripts

1.10 All hearings were recorded on audio. Transcripts of these audio recordings are available from the Commission office upon request.

Exhibits

1.11 There were a total of 391 Exhibits produced. A list of the Exhibits appears in Appendix 1. The documents exhibited are all available at the office of the Commission but for ease of reference some of these documents will be attached where particular matters are referred to in this report. In addition some documents and correspondences were sent from overseas but the sender did not appear. Also because some witnesses were overseas we found it more convenient that the questions and answers be made in writing. All these documents appear in Appendix 2 and 3. These include correspondences with the former Acting Governor of Vava'u, Tu'a Taumoepeau, (Appendix 2) and correspondences with the Hon. Minister of Lands, Lord Tuita and his CEO Dr Nailasikau Halatuituia (Appendix 3)

CHAPTER 2 - REAL ESTATE AGENTS

Definition

2.1 A Real Estate Agent can be defined as a person whose business is dealing with land especially with the buying and selling of land for which he gets a commission or fee for the services he renders. As such, the Agent is a type of middleman who connects the landowner and the buyer/tenant.

Introduction of Real Estate Agents

2.2 The business of Real Estate Agents was first introduced to Vava'u by a person named Robert Bryce in 2004/2005. Unfortunately Mr. Bryce relocated his business to Fiji in 2008 and the Commission was not able to have him give evidence. However, the Commission considered evidence about his work in Vava'u through clients and people who had worked with him who gave evidence. He still conducts his real estate business in respect of land in Vava'u from Fiji.

Means of conducting business

2.3 Robert Bryce conducted his business through advertisements on a website in the internet. The website he used was www.southpacificrealestate.to. The website would give a description of the land, its location, pictures, term available in years and the price payable. A sample of information and listings in this website is shown in Exhibit 311.

Show of interest

2.4 The advertisements on the internet were aimed at and drew interests from foreigners most of whom had never visited Tonga. These people had money which they wished to invest for their future or simply to relocate to a place which they would feel their "dream home" away from home. Most saw this as an opportunity to begin a business relating mainly to tourism through which they would get a fair return and hopefully a profit for their investment.

2.5 The advertisements also drew interests from persons who had aspirations of setting up their own Real Estate Agent businesses.

Means of Communication

2.6 All initial communications and correspondences were conducted through the internet between the Real Estate Agent and the client. At other times a Commission Agent who would find and introduce the landowner to the Real Estate Agent would also be involved. The Tongan land owner was almost never involved with the client and his interest would only be in the receipt of the upfront money due to him under the Agreement and the monthly payment for rent. Sometimes a client would visit Tonga and would meet the landowner but this was not essential for the purpose of the agreement.

New Real Estate Agents

2.7 All the new Real Estate Agents were initially attracted to Vava'u through the website advertisements made by Robert Bryce. Their initial contacts were to show interest in a particular site advertised and either took it or decided to do their own business after getting some contacts and advice in Tonga.

2.8 The first new Real Estate Agent to set up business in Vava'u was Mr. Nesha Rosic in 2005. He made an application and was issued a Professional Services Licence by the Vava'u office of the Ministry of Labour, Commerce and Industries. This Licence indicated that it allowed Rosic to conduct the business of a Real Estate Agent. Mr. Rosic is married to a Tongan woman and continues his real estate business in Vava'u up to now. He advertises under the website www.vavaurealestate.com and a sample of his listings (advertisements) is attached as Appendix 4.

2.9 The second new Real Estate Agent who came to Vava'u was Mr. Trevor Jefferson from Missouri, U.S.A. He arrived in Vava'u in January 2005 as a pastor, freelance writer and a Real Estate Agent. He was first attracted by the website of Robert Bryce. He set up his own website, www.investintonga.com, and carried on his business as a Real Estate Agent. There is no evidence that he got a Real Estate Agent Licence to practice that trade and all that he had was a Business Visa. He worked more with Robert Bryce and showed dislike and animosity towards Nesha Rosic.

2.10 The third new Real Estate Agent to set up business in Vava'u was Mr. Gordon Allison. He was attracted by the website advertisements of both Mr. Bryce and Mr. Rosic. He came to Vava'u in December 2006 initially as a buyer/investor but developed into a Real Estate Agent through his sales of sites on lease which he advertises. A sample of his advertisements is attached as Appendix 5. Ultimately Mr. Rosic and Mr. Allison worked together in the promotion and development of their Real Estate business in opposition to those of Mr. Bryce. Mr. Allison continues his Real Estate business in Vava'u up to now.

Competition

2.11 The available land for the Vava'u market is limited. Invariably the Real Estate Agents found themselves involved in the same piece of land with the same Tongan landowner. Competition became fierce in particular between Bryce and Jefferson on the one side and Rosic and Allison on the other side. Allegations of fraud and illegal dealings were made against each other on the internet through the use of various websites. A sample is shown in Exhibit 127, 128 and 129. Derogatory and defamatory emails were sent from various sources alleging fraud and illegal activities by one or the other of these Agents. Land officials in the Vava'u office and Tongan lawyers were dragged into these allegations. Robert Bryce made allegations of property damage and threats of physical violence to him and his family by Nesha Rosic that finally made up his mind to leave Tonga in fear for their safety and relocated his business in Fiji. Prior to doing so however, he was sued by Gordon Allison for defamation which the police prosecuted as a criminal defamation. The case was dismissed because of the lack of evidence and the key witness who was alleged to have received the defamatory email did not appear. Trevor Jefferson also alleged in evidence that Nesha Rosic threatened him physically in a Chinese shop in Neiafu.

Moratorium on Real Estate Licences

2.12 Evidence was received from the Officer in Charge in Vava'u of the office of the Ministry of Labour, Commerce and Industries, Ms Sapate Toke, that a moratorium on the issuance of Real Estate Service Licences was conveyed to her from Head Office in Nuku'alofa to be effected from March 2007. This moratorium was conveyed to her verbally and since March 2007 she has abided by it and has not issued any Real Estate Licence. The current Business Licences Act came into effect in 2007 and provides for all the businesses that can be practiced in Tonga and which require a licence to be issued under that Act and kept current annually before a person can carry out that business. Real Estate Service Licence is one of the businesses covered by that Act that require a licence after application and on the payment of a fee and renewed annually to allow anyone to practice that trade in Tonga. The moratorium on Real Estate Service Licences since March 2007 meant that no such licences were issued by the Vava'u office since that date. This was confirmed by the Officer in Charge. She also issued a letter with respect to Nesha Rosic at the request of the Governor of Vava'u and a copy is shown as Exhibit 96. In spite of having no Real Estate Agent Licence as required by the Business Licences Act, all persons practicing as real estate agents have continued their trade in Vava'u in disregard of the law and with impunity. It is obvious that the Ministry responsible for the issuance of these licences is aware of the moratorium and the unlawful practice of the real estate agents in Vava'u but has failed to instigate prosecution for the offence as directed by the Act.

2.13 As a matter of courtesy a letter was written to the Minister of Labour, Commerce and Industries informing him of what was happening in Vava'u (Appendix 6).

2.14 In his evidence, the Minister for Labour Commerce and Industries, Hon. Lisiate 'Akolo confirmed that he had issued the direction to stop the issuance of Real Estate Licences as from March 2007 and that this direction was still effective up to now. In a letter of complaint to the Minister from a person named Graham Gibson dated 4 March 2009 Mr. Gibson said that he was aware "that Mr Rosic did not have a current Real Estate Licence" and that "the Ministry should be actively investigating Mr. Rosic's activities in order to protect the interests of the public and prosecuting him in accordance with the provisions of the Business Licence Act for carrying on a business without a business licence." When this was put to the Minister and why no action was taken on what appeared to be a breach of the law that he was responsible to enforce his answer was that it was mo'ungaloa – just forgotten. The letter from Mr Gibson is found in Exhibit 56B.

2.15 The Minister for Labour Commerce and Industries was also shown a copy of a Real Estate Licence that was issued to Mana'ia Real Estate on the 1st February 2010 expiring on the 31st December 2010 (Exhibit 314). This was issued in Tongatapu from the Minister's office. This was obviously issued contrary to the moratorium that the Minister issued in March 2007 but the Minister did not know that his own office was still issuing such licences. The Minister undertook to check this matter and also the moratorium itself and its relevance now.

2.16 The owner of Mana'ia Real Estate, Ms Monalisa Palu in evidence revealed that her business started in 2007 and her licence has been renewed every year since. A copy of the Real Estate Services Licence issued to Mana'ia Real Estate are shown for 2007 (Exhibit 330), 2008 (Exhibit 332) and 2009 (Exhibit 340).

2.17 In 2008 Ms Christine 'Uta'atu applied for a Real Estate Services Licence on behalf of her company, Pacific Property Development Company Limited to the Ministry of Labour Commerce and Industries. The licence was denied because of the direction that been issued by the Minister in 2007. In a letter dated 15 April 2008 to the Secretary of the Ministry, Exhibit 333, Ms 'Uta'atu pointed out that denying her company the licence was contrary to the provisions of the Business Licence Act 2002 and Regulations. A licence was subsequently issued to Pacific Property Development Co. Ltd for 2008 and it is shown in Exhibit 325. This licence was renewed in 2009 and 2010.

2.18 In his evidence, Sione Vailanu, Deputy Secretary of the Ministry of Labour, Commerce and Industries said that the moratorium on the issue of Real Estate Services was made because the land deals made by foreigners resulted in their getting more money than the Tongan landowner. In spite of the moratorium, he issued the licences in Tongatapu in respect only of "house rentals" and with the approval of the Minister. This is evident from the licence issued in 2009 and 2010 to Pacific Property Development Co. Ltd (Exhibit 325) where the words "House Rental" are inserted under the business activity of Real Estate Services. The owner of the licence simply ignored this purported restriction as she was of the opinion that there was no authority for it in the Business Licences Act.

2.19 While the Ministry was issuing licences in Tongatapu, it did not inform the office in Vava'u which continued to enforce the moratorium and refused all applications for a Real Estate Service Licence.

2.20 The Commission recommends that the Minister for Labour, Commerce and Industries reconsider the reason, justification and usefulness of the moratorium he issued effective from March 2007 stopping the issuance of Real Estate Services Licences. He should also ensure that his Ministry act within the provisions of the Business Licences Act 2002 in the issuance of licences and apply the same standard throughout the whole of Tonga. Something needs to be done immediately to ensure that both Tongatapu and Vava'u are given and act within the same directions from Head Office. Those continuing their real estate businesses in Vava'u in spite of the moratorium and having no such licence should be investigated subject to the question of the validity of the moratorium in light of the Business Licences Act or any other law in Tonga.

Commission Agent

2.21 Another person involved in the real estate business in Vava'u but from a perceived different angle is Mr. Hans Schmeiser. He is of Austrian origin and came to Tonga in 1982, operated a number of tourist businesses including the Hilltop Hotel, married a Tongan lady, became naturalized as a Tongan in 1994 and has lived in Vava'u up to now.

2.22 Hans Schmeiser operates under a Commission Agent Licence which gives him a commission on every business related deal that he is involved in. He quickly teamed up with Robert Bryce in the Real Estate business. Schmeiser worked with a Tongan, Peau Halahingano who was responsible for acting as an interpreter to the Tongan landowner. Schmeiser's work and reputation became known in Vava'u. Tongan landowners who wanted money for their land approached him to find a client who is willing to take the land for the payment of money. Schmeiser would inform the landowner to retain a part of his land for his own use and give up only a part on the coast for the money payment. The sum that the landowner would get is agreed and the remainder would go to Schmeiser for his commission and other expenses.

2.23 Schmeiser operated two forms of agreement. One was the "Aleapau Ngaue" in the Tongan language setting out the description of the land, the amount of money that the landowner would get, the monthly rental, and the amount of the commission payable to Schmeiser. This agreement was made between Schmeiser and the landowner and was explained to the landowner by Peau Halahingano and later by a Tongan lawyer and was signed by the landowner and Schmeiser. The other agreement was a Tenancy Agreement in the English language between the landowner and yet to be found tenant reflecting the terms of the Aleapau Ngaue. The Tenancy Agreement is then taken to a Tongan lawyer who explains the terms to the Tongan landowner who then signs the agreement in the presence of the lawyer. Sometimes the wife of the landowner and their eldest son also sign the agreement as possible future successors. Both these agreements will be discussed in more detail and examples given in the next chapter of this report.

2.24 Schmeiser would then take the Tenancy Agreement to Robert Bryce to look for a tenant through advertising in his website. Once a tenant is found, an unsigned copy of the Tenancy Agreement is sent by Schmeiser to the tenant and if he agrees to the terms and pays the upfront money required by the agreement, Schmeiser then sends two copies of the Tenancy Agreement that was signed by the landlord to the tenant for signing and returning one copy to Schmeiser. Under the agreement the payment of the upfront money is to be made to an account name Island Escrow with the ANZ Bank which is operated by Schmeiser while the monthly rent is payable to an account of the landlord. The commission for Robert Bryce is also payable from the upfront money.

2.25 Schmeiser does not have a website like Bryce and the other Real Estate Agents. However, from the description of the work done by him with the two agreements with the landowner, the contract made with the tenant and the receipt of the money to the Escrow Account operated by him, he would appear to be carrying out the function of a Real Estate Agent as well as that of a Commission Agent. The Ministry of Labour, Commerce and Industries would need to look at this carefully to see that appropriate licences are applied for and given to cover these separate occupations under the Business Licences Act 2002.

Tongatapu Real Estate Agents

2.26 A few real estate agents conducted business in Tongatapu. They were mainly Tongan nationals and they were summonsed and gave evidence in Nuku'alofa. The earliest, Hasdra Real Estate began in 2004.

2.27 Those who carried on real estate business in Tongatapu and who gave evidence were, Hasdra Real Estate (Mr. Hasting Fa'apoi), Pacific Property Development Co. Ltd (Ms Christine 'Uta'atu), Mana'ia Real Estate (Ms Monalisa Palu), Market Tonga Real Estate (Ms Vao'ese Kava) and Niu Real Estate (Ms Dana Stephenson). Hasdra Real Estate closed its operation in 2009 and was replaced by Capital Realty operated by the same owner, Hasting Fa'apoi. Ms Dana Stephenson ended her involvement with Niu Real Estate in 2009.

2.28 From the evidence received, it appeared that the Tongatapu Real Estate Agents did not have the same problems that involved the Vava'u Real Estate Agents. The business in Tongatapu involved the more traditional short term renting of houses or leasing of land and sale of leaseholds. There was no long term tenancy agreement or lease agreement like those used in Vava'u.

2.29 As noticed above when discussing the moratorium on the issuance of real estate licences they continued to be issued to Real Estate Agents in Tongatapu on the basis that it was only for house rental. Vava'u was not informed of this so the officer in charge continued the moratorium up to now. As we have seen however, Real Estate Agents in Vava'u continue their business without a licence.

Ha'apai Land Deals

2.30 There were only two land deals in Ha'apai that came to our notice. One was included in the advertisements by Nesha Rosic that was downloaded from the website www.vavaurealestate.com in Uonuku Island (Exhibit 242) that included two properties. When Rosic gave evidence these properties had not yet been leased. Presumably, when a tenant is found, the lease agreement Rosic used in the Vava'u deals would be used. The other was in relation to a property in Ha'apai that was brought to our notice by David Corbett in his evidence where he provided an email exchange with a client, Vera Velanova (Exhibit 387). This was in relation to a property in Ha'apai marketed by a real estate agent in Vava'u where a sum of money was paid as deposit to the Ha'apai land owner Mr Peleketi. Apparently, a higher offer was made by the Tongatapu real estate agent Market Tonga and advertised in their website listing No. L525.

CHAPTER 3 - AGREEMENTS USED BY REAL ESTATE AGENTS

3.1 It quickly became apparent to the Real Estate Agents in Vava'u that the land law of Tonga has many aspects that are different from those that they are used to in their own respective countries. Tonga does not have freehold land. The sale of land is forbidden under the Constitution and the Land Act. Leasehold may be sold but that is only for the remaining term of years of that lease. There is also a limitation on the number of years that land may be leased, and in respect of a Tax Allotment, this is only 20 years with an option of renewal for another 10 years. There are also strict rules of succession to land.

3.2 Real Estate Agents became quite knowledgeable with Tongan land law. This was apparent in their evidence when they confidently referred to land law and case law on Tongan land in their answers to questions. It also became apparent that Real Estate Agents were giving advice on Tongan land law when answering queries from clients with or without the help of Tongan lawyers.

3.3 The result of this knowledge of land law was seen and expressed in the agreements used by Real Estate Agents in their endeavour to comply with or circumvent the strict requirements of Tongan land law. The first of these agreements was the Tenancy Agreement used by Hans Schmeiser and Gordon Bryce with the help of Laki Niu. Others followed with some variations.

Tenancy Agreement

3.4 The Tenancy Agreement drafted by Laki Niu and used by Robert Bryce had the following features:
a) It was an agreement between the landowner, his wife and eldest son, and the tenant;
b) The tenant agrees to construct buildings on an identified part of the property of the landowner;
c) Upon construction of the buildings, they become owned by the landlord;
d) The landlord then rents these buildings to the tenant under the Tenancy Agreement;

e) A substantial upfront amount of money in US dollars is paid by the tenant on signing the Tenancy Agreement to a bank account nominated by the agent;
f) The upfront payment includes the money agreed to be paid to the landowner and the commission of the agent;
g) A smaller monthly payment in US dollars is payable to the bank account of thelandlord;
h) The term of the Tenancy Agreement was normally for a period of between 50 years to 99 years with a right of renewal and of assignment. A sample of this Tenancy Agreement is shown in Exhibit 44.

3.5 It was noted that the first Tenancy Agreement used by Robert Bryce and Hans Schmeiser was worded that the "premises" that were the subject of the agreement were "the buildings etc which were to be constructed and the land upon which the buildings are constructed". A sample of this agreement is found in Exhibit 33. The agreement has the seal and signature of Laki Niu indicating that it was drafted by him. Laki Niu confirmed this in his evidence.

3.6 A later version changed this to what is seen in Exhibit 44 to say that the "premises" that are the subject of the agreement are "the buildings etc which were to be constructed upon the land" which is then identified. The subtle difference in the wording is important and obviously recognized as such by the drafter because of the interpretation that was given to the Tenancy Agreement as outlined in the next paragraph. Although not carrying the seal and signature of Laki Niu, he produced a template that was the same thus indicating that he was also responsible for the drafting of this agreement.

3.7 All the lands that were the subject of these Tenancy Agreements were part of tax allotments. They would therefore be subject to the restriction on leasing to 20 years. It is argued that the Tenancy Agreement outlined above is not an agreement for the lease of land as the land remains the property of the landowner. The buildings on the land are also owned by the landowner. What the landowner has agreed to under the Tenancy Agreement is to rent his own buildings to the tenant. It is therefore a purely commercial agreement for the occupancy of buildings that would be subject to the normal commercial law and the laws of contract. It is argued therefore that the land law of Tonga does not apply to the Tenancy Agreement so the restrictions under the Tongan land law do not apply. This meant that the 20 years restriction on leasing of a tax allotment or part thereof does not apply to the Tenancy Agreement with its term of over 50 years because this was not a lease of land. A letter from Laki Niu expressing his opinion on the Tenancy Agreement is found in Exhibit 37.

3.8 In his evidence, Laki Niu also expressed the view that the Tenancy Agreement is binding on all who sign it. In the case of Exhibit 44 this would mean the registered owner, his wife and their eldest son. This is in order to bind all the immediate prospective heirs. It was also indicated by Laki Niu that when these parties die the Tenancy Agreement would terminate even though on paper it may have more years to run. This would appear to the Commission to be quite misleading to the tenant and there was no evidence to show that they were informed of this when they entered the Tenancy Agreement or were aware of this limitation to the life of those who signed the agreement instead of the term of years indicated in the Tenancy Agreement. Such an important term should be clearly stated in the agreement to inform the tenant who in most cases was residing in a foreign country.

3.9 A contrary view and interpretation says that the Tenancy Agreement is void and illegal. This is based on the general principles and meaning of Tongan land and of the protections it is aimed to afford to Tongans. The strict requirements of Section 13 of the Land Act are raised. This forbids any dealing with land outside the provisions of the Land Act, unless approved in writing by the Minister of Lands, and deems such dealings as illegal and subject to a monetary fine penalty. This view is fully expressed by Kahungunu BarronAfeaki, in his capacity as a legal counsel at the time in his report that was made in December 2007 for his clients and given to Government. A copy of this report is found in Exhibit 24.

3.10 The different interpretations and contrary views expressed on the validity of the Tenancy Agreement can only be solved by a court of law or by legislation. No one has taken this matter to the courts yet.

3.11 The CEO of the Ministry of Lands informed the Commission of the Ministry's position and that it recognizes the 5-year agreement for farming purposes as has been done for decades, but it does not recognize tenancy agreements. He suggests that the legality and validity of tenancy agreements need to be clearly defined (refer to Letter dated 24 May 2010 in Appendix 3).

3.12 The Commission consider it necessary that Government provide legislation to cover tenancy agreements and for their registration. It is important that tenancy agreements, especially for lengthy periods, are registered so that the public has notice of this when they are dealing with or are interested in that land. It will also serve to protect the interests of the parties as recorded in any such agreement. Government may also consider the length of the term of tenancy agreements and perhaps remove the restriction of the 20 years term that a tax allotment to allow a longer term that would encourage land developers to construct tourist facilities that would help develop the economy of Tonga. Aleapau Ngaue

3.13 In conjunction with the Tenancy Agreement, Hans Schmeiser had an agreement in Tongan called "Aleapau

Ngaue". A sample is found in Exhibit 79. This is the first agreement that the Tongan landholder commits himself to and it is between Hans Schmeiser and the landlord. Basically what this agreement does is to commit the land to Schmeiser to find a tenant in advance of the Tenancy Agreement. It also states the amount of money that the landlord will get upfront and the monthly rental and the commission of Hans Schmeiser. Once the Tenancy Agreement is signed then this Aleapau Ngaue ceases. This Aleapau Ngaue is explained to the landowner by the Tongan helper of Schmeiser who was usually Peau Halahingano and was drafted with the help of a Tongan lawyer, To'imoana Taufateau. Offer and Counter Offer

3.14 This is another form of agreement that was used by Nesha Rosic. It is peculiar in that Nesha Rosic represents both the landlord and the tenant. The offer is made from the tenant to the landlord where Rosic represents the tenant. This offer sets out the price and other monetary considerations for the use of the land under a Tenancy Agreement. The counter offer is from the landlord to the tenant where Rosic represents the landlord.

Offer and Counter Offer

3.14 This is another form of agreement that was used by Nesha Rosic. It is peculiar in that Nesha Rosic represents both the landlord and the tenant. The offer is made from the tenant to the landlord where Rosic represents the tenant. This offer sets out the price and other monetary considerations for the use of the land under a Tenancy Agreement. The counter offer is from the landlord to the tenant where Rosic represents the landlord. It is not certain why the offer and acceptance were made but we can only assume that it was a way of committing the landlord to an agreement which would later be firmed up with the Tenancy Agreement. A sample of the Offer and Counter Offer is attached as Appendix 7.

Lease Agreement

3.15 Nesha Rosic and Gordon Allison used a lease agreement with their clients that was signed by the landholder, his wife and eldest son. This agreement usually gave the tenant/lessee a term of 50 years with an option to renew for another 49 years. It also had a substantial upfront payment, commission for the agent plus a monthly rental payable to the landowner. Gordon Allison referred to this agreement in evidence as a "family agreement" meaning that it was an agreement that was binding on the family in spite of it being for a term that is beyond that allowed by law of 20 years for a tax allotment.

3.16 In a letter to Hans Schmeiser dated 20 June 2007 Laki Niu gave the opinion that this lease agreement was illegal and void. The basis for this opinion was that the Land Act 26 prohibited the lease of a tax allotment or part thereof for more than 20 years with an option to renew for another 10 years. In addition under section 13 of the Land Act it was illegal to deal with land in any manner contrary to that provided in the Act. A copy of this letter and opinion is found in Exhibit 37A.

3.17 Dana Stephenson held similar views with Laki Niu on the illegality of the lease/family agreement. She advised a client of this and took the matter up with the New Zealand Estate Agents Authority as advertisements were made in a NZ Real Estate circular offering these properties for the term of 50 plus 49 years. A copy of Ms Stephenson's letter to the NZ Estates Agent Authority and the response are found in Exhibits 56G and 56H respectively. The decision of the NZ Estates Agent Authority on the complaint dated the 23rd March 2010 is found in Exhibit 371. Although Ms. Stephenson does not agree with the decision she had formed the view that it was not worthwhile appealing.

3.18 In evidence Trevor Jefferson claimed that he also operated a lease agreement for over 20 years of tax allotments but it provided that when an L.9 form application is made for 20 years and registered, his lease agreement becomes void. It is difficult to see how a tenant who takes a lease for 50 years can agree to the reduction of that term to 20 years by the use of the L.9 form. A sample of the Jefferson lease agreement is found in Exhibit 227 but it does not contain any provision to terminate in the event of a successful L9 application for a lease.

3.19 In addition to the lease agreement/family agreement Allison and Rosic required the landowner and his family to sign an application for a lease in Government L.9 form of the same property for the legal term of 20 years. The idea was that a legal lease would be granted over the property for the term of 20 years while at the same time the family would be bound by the lease/family agreement for the term stated therein so that the lease would in effect run for 50 plus 49 years. Allison in evidence said that he was given advice that because of the drive to encourage more tourists to Tonga, once tourist facilities and buildings were constructed, Government would allow the terms of the lease/family agreement to continue. Both Nesha Rosic and Gordon Allison may have been encouraged along this line of thinking by the advice Rosic received from Ms Rosamond Bing (email dated 13 July 2007 Exhibit 103). A sample copy of the L9 lease application form is found in Exhibit 30.

3.20 It is noted that the difference between the lease/family agreement and the Tenancy Agreement is that the lease/family agreement is over land while the Tenancy Agreement is over buildings built on land which become owned by the landowner who does not part 27 with his land ownership. In his evidence however, Laki Niu said that the Tenancy Agreement he drafted included the land upon which the building rests. It must also include access to the building through the land of the owner. Pita Hala'api'api-Toula, Vava'u

3.21 Pita Hala'api'api worked closely with Robert Bryce since 2004. Even when Bryce departed Tonga in 2008 to set up his business in Fiji, they continued working together in that Pita's properties and those of other people were marketed by Bryce through his website.

3.22 Pita had his own property in Toula which he subdivided and marketed using Lafi Moetala Development which became the development body (landowner) who made the Tenancy Agreement with the investor/tenant.

3.23 The first agreement is the Agreement for Services and Participation in Lafi Moetala Development between the landholder and Pita and Bryce (Agent) (Exhibit 169). This agreement gives the land to the Agent to find an investor for 99 years with an up-front payment of not less than TOP$3000 and also says that the landowner will receive in Pa'anga the same numeral as the price in US Dollar from each investor. The difference is kept by the agent for commission and expenses.

3.24 The next stage is when an investor is found. A Landholder and Investor/Plot-Holder Agreement is made (Exhibit 250). This is the tenancy agreement which sets out the term of 99 years and a monthly rental of US$88, the one-time fee having already been paid. The monthly rent is reviewed every 15 years and a fee of US$120 is payable on the transfer of the agreement.

3.25 The Lafi Moetala Devdelopment project was set up by Pita Hala'api'api and Robert Bryce to market Pita's land and also the land of those living in Toula. It was a type of cooperative help for the community in finance and development. Other villages like Tu'anuku followed suit with their own Development projects (Exhibit 273)

CHAPTER 4 - NUAPAPU ISLAND AGREEMENTS

4.1 The inevitable conflict between the Tenancy Agreement of Bryce and Schmeiser and the Lease Agreement of Rosic and Allison came to a head over land in the island of Nuapapu. Houmatoka and Lolovi

4.2 There were two tax allotments in Nuapapu Island, one Houmatoka registered by Moleni Fe'aomoeata ("Moleni") and the other Lolovi registered by his son Moleni Fonokalafi Fe'aomoeata ("Fonokalafi"). Moleni died in 1999 and his son Fonokalafi as heir elected under section 84 of the Land Act to take his father's tax allotment – Houmatoka – and give his tax allotment – Lolovi – to his son Piea. This election was registered with the Governor's office and is found in Exhibit 15. It took sometimes for this choice to be effected but in 2005 the Deed of Title of Houmatoka was endorsed and signed by the Acting Governor showing Moleni Fonokalafi as the registered holder. This Deed with the endorsement made by the Acting Governor on the 7th December 2005 is found in Exhibit 12. The Registration Book did not record this and he was still recorded as the owner of Lolovi. To complicate matters more, the Acting Governor had endorsed the Deed of Lolovi to Moleni Fonokalafi on the 29th November 2005 when it should have been given to Piea because of the election made by Moleni Fonokalafi. This Deed of Lolovi including the endorsement of the Acting Governor dated the 29th November 2005 is found in Exhibit 21. On the 29th June 2007 Piea Fe'aomoeata is entered in the Registration Book as the owner of Houmatoka while his father Moleni Fonokalafi, the registered owner of the allotment was still alive. This was done by the Land Registration Officer Makafilia Mafi on instruction from the Acting Governor. In November 2007 an entry made by Land

Registration Officer Fataua Halatanu in the book recording matters over land and directions by the Acting Governor stated that the Acting Governor wanted the question over Piea's name in the Registration Book to be clarified with Makafilia Mafi before any further deals are made with regard to this land.

4.3 Both the Acting Governor Tu'a Taumoepeau and the Land Registration Officer Makafilia Mafi have a lot of explaining to give over the registration of Houmatoka and Lolovi. Makafilia was dismissed from his job before our inquiry and Tu'a is in New York. We got some answers from Makafilia in his evidence but he puts the ball back with the Governor claiming he was only doing what the Governor had directed. We have asked questions by email to Tu'a but it is difficult to get reliable evidence by this means. A copy of the email correspondences with Tu'a are attached as Appendix 2. It appears from this correspondence that the Governor relied heavily on the advice of his Land Registration Officer, Makafilia Mafi.

4.4 As a result of correspondence with the former Acting Governor of Vava'u, Tu'a Taumoepeau (Appendix 2), the Commission received a copy of an Internal Memorandum dated 15 May 2007 (Appendix 8) from Makafilia Mafi to the Governor. This Memorandum stated that –

a) Houmatoka was registered by Moleni Fe'aomoeata in 1930;

b) Moleni Fe'aomoeata died in 1999 and his son Moleni Fonokalafi Fe'aomoeata claimed this property as heir;

c) In 2005, Moleni Fe'aomoeata had an agreement with Richard Mortimer and Eric Stark in relation to Houmatoka instead of Lolovi which was registered under his name;

d) The deed of grant of Houmatoka showed that this property was inherited by Moleni Fonokalafi Fe'aomoeata as heir in 2005, but this was wrong because it was not entered in the Registration Book;

e) Houmatoka should have first been transferred to Moleni Fonokalafi Fe'aomoeata or Piea Fe'aomoeata as the heir before the agreements with Mortimer and Stark.

4.5 A note from the Governor dated 12 June 2007 said to "Transfer Land in Question to Piea Fe'aomoeata (Legal Heir)".

4.6 What is missing from the Memorandum by Makafilia is that Moleni Fonokalafi Fe'aomoeata had made the election allowed to him by the Land Act to inherit his father's allotment (Houmatoka) and give his allotment (Lolovi) to his son Piea.

Dealings with Houmatoka

4.7 In 2005 the registered owner of a tax allotment (Houmatoka) in Nuapapu Island, Moleni Fonokalafi Fe'aomoeata contacted Hans Schmeiser seeking a tenant for his allotment. On the 13th December 2005 an agreement in the form of the Aleapau Ngaue was entered into between Moleni Fonokalafi Fe'aomoeata and Hans Schmeiser in respect of 4 acres of the allotment. This agreement gave Schmeiser the right to seek a tenant for the land within 24 months. The term of years was 60 years and the landowner Moleni Fonokalafi Fe'aomoeata was to receive US$35,000 plus US$300 per month. We received only the first page of this Aleapau Ngaue from Schmeiser a copy of which is found in Exhibit 78.

4.8 On the 16th February 2006 a Tenancy Agreement was made between Moleni, his wife Tupou and son Piea as Landlord and Richard Mortimer of Hong Kong as Tenant for the "buildings, fences and structures, which exist or are to be built in pursuance of this Agreement and upon the land which is described on the map or description page attached hereto". The land is then described with an area of 2 acres of the allotment. The term is for 60 years and the rent is stated to be

US$28,965 payable upon signing plus a monthly rent of US$70. A copy of this Tenancy Agreement is found in Exhibit 44.

4.9 On the 1st December 2006 Moleni, his wife Tupou and son Piea entered into another Tenancy Agreement with Eric Stark of Hong Kong (a friend of Richard Mortimer) over the "buildings, fences and structures" etc as in the Mortimer agreement. The land involved has an area of 2 acres adjoining that in the agreement with Mortimer. The term is 60 years and the rent is US$27,200 payable upon signing plus a monthly rent of US$70. A copy of this Tenancy Agreement is found in Exhibit 35.

4.10 Both 2 acre allotments were believed to be on the coast of the 7 acre allotment of Moleni Fonokalafi Fe'aomoeata. There is also evidence of this in the maps and plans produced. A copy of a plan signed by Moleni and the tenant is found in Exhibit 45.

4.11 We received evidence that all money due under both Tenancy Agreements were paid in accordance with the terms of the agreement and some of the monthly rent were paid in advance (Exhibits 1, 2, 5, 57A, 57B, 78 and 305).

4.12 In January 2007 Moleni Fe'aomoeata went to the surveyor Paula Moa Lo'amanu to cancel the scheme plan of his allotment which showed that the allotments concerned with the Tenancy Agreements with Mortimer and Stark were on the coast. He wanted to cancel this scheme plan. Paula took the matter up with Hans Schmeiser and cancelled the scheme plan as requested by Moleni and re-drew a new scheme plan that showed the 4 acres that were for Mortimer and Stark had only one 2 acre coastal area. Paula Moa in evidence claimed that he did not know about the Tenancy Agreements with Mortimer and Stark - if he did, he would not have altered the scheme plan as requested by Moleni. A copy of the scheme plan with the entry signed by Moleni to cancel is found in Exhibit 132.

4.13 On the 16th January 2007 an application for a lease in the L.9 Government form was signed by Moleni Fonokalafi Fe'aomoeata in favour of a company named Escape Tonga Limited whose principals were Gordon Allison and Peter Glover over a 3 acre area that included the 2 acre land that were already subject to the Tenancy Agreement with Richard Mortimer. A copy of this application is found in Exhibit 83. 31

4.14 On the 1st February 2007 Moleni, his wife Tupou and son Piea entered into a Lease Agreement (Exhibit 80) with Gordon Allison and Peter Glover for the 3 acre plot of land referred to in the previous paragraph of which 2 acres were the subject of the Tenancy Agreement with Richard Mortimer. This lease is for 50 years with an option to renew for another 49 years. The total rent is US$125,000 with a down payment of US$35,000 upon Cabinet approval of the lease and yearly payments of US$2,000 for 50 years. This is the agreement that Gordon Allison referred to as the "Family Agreement" in his evidence as opposed to the Government approved lease.

4.15 In his evidence, Heilala Fe'aomoeata who is a younger brother of Piea Fe'aomoeata, produced an agreement dated 21 July 2007 (Exhibit 324) which was given to him by Nesha Rosic. This agreement was the same as Exhibit 80 but the lessor party was shown as Piea Fe'aomoeata instead of his father Moleni who was still alive at the time. This would coincide with the fact that Piea's name was entered in the Registration book as the owner of Houmatoka on the 29th June 2007 (Exhibit 14).

4.16 A similar agreement was entered into by the Moleni family and Nesha Rosic on the 1st February 2007 over the remaining 4 acres that included the 2 acres which was the subject of the Tenancy Agreement with Eric Stark. A copy of this agreement is found in Exhibit 109.

4.17 Correspondences were exchanged between Robert Bryce and Nesha Rosic over the double dealing with the same land. Rosic's answer was basically that the Tenancy Agreement had lapsed because of the non-payment of rent and that Allison's lease agreement and his were valid as the land was vacant. There was no record of the Tenancy Agreement in the Land office as there was no requirement to register such agreements with the Ministry of Land. An email to this effect dated 29 September 2007 was sent by Samiu Vaipulu to Eric Stark and Richard Mortimer (Exhibit 106).

4.18 On the 29th June 2007 both Gordon Allison and Nesha Rosic signed two separate L.9 lease applications on behalf of their respective company, Escape Tonga Ltd and Island Real Estate Ltd, for 20 years over the 3 acres and 4 acres land in Nuapapu of Moleni's family the subject of the present discussion. This was signed by Piea Fe'aomoeata as the landowner and his name was entered in the Land Registration Book as the holder on the same day. Piea's father who held the Deed of Title for this land was still alive at the time. A copy of the death certificate of Moleni Fonokalafi Fe'aomoeata who died on the 28th October 2008 is found in Exhibit 19. There is a cloud hanging over the entry of Piea in the 32 Registration Book by the Registration Officer Makafilia Mafi and approved by the Acting Governor Tu'a Taumoepeau. Some explanation is seen in the Internal Memorandum dated 15 May 2007 from Makafilia Mafi to the Governor (Appendix 8) but the cloud still hangs. A copy of the L.9 application for lease by Gordon Allison and Nesha Rosic are found in Exhibits 30 and 31 respectively.

4.19 On advice from Robert Bryce to show his right to the land, Richard Mortimer arranged for the construction of a water tank in September 2007 on the land over which he had a Tenancy Agreement with the Moleni family. As soon as it was constructed, Nesha Rosic arranged for some Tongans to destroy the water tank and this was done. Richard Mortimer made a written complaint to the police which was given to the OIC in Vava'u CIP Sisi Tonga who passed it on to the Falevai branch to see if it was an offence that should involve the police (Exhibit 120).

4.20 The Falevai Police Station Diary (Exhibit 391) shows that the complaint for the destruction of the water tank was made by the builder, Manu Tu'itupou on the 21st September 2007. The diary records police investigation and a charge being made against Kineleti Taufa on the 19th November 2007 in respect of the destruction of the water tank. The Diary also shows that on the 30th April 2008 a Case Disposition Notice was signed by the complainant Manu Tu'itupou withdrawing his complaint because a civil case had been taken out. The Diary also shows an entry made on the 16th December 2008 recording a direction from the Officer in Charge of Police Station No. 5 to re-open the case. There was a change of OIC in Falevai Station and the file was handed over to LCPL Latu. No further entry was recorded in the Diary for 2009 and the only work recorded in 2010 was in respect of the production of the Station Diary to the Commission.

4.21 On advice from a Tonga lawyer, Kelepi Piukala, a court proceeding was brought by the person who constructed the water tank against Rosic and those who destroyed the water tank. The Magistrate gave judgment for the plaintiff tank builder (Exhibit 6) but on appeal, the Supreme Court gave judgment for the defendants who were responsible for the destruction on the basis that the proper party was the owner of the tank Richard Mortimer and that the case was brought by the wrong party, namely the builder. As seen from the judgment of Andrew J in the Supreme Court (Exhibit 7) the

Judge said that another ground for the success of the appeal was that the property was the subject of a registered leased to Escape Tonga Ltd, the company of Gordon Allison. No mention was made of the prior Tenancy Agreement of Richard Mortimer over the same land. No mention was made also of the fact that when the water tank was destroyed there was no lease registered over the land. In his evidence, Kelepi Piukala failed to satisfy us that he had produced the Tenancy Agreement as evidence in the appeal. If he had, the Judge would have commented on it and given a ruling on its validity. The chance for an interpretation by the court of the Tenancy Agreement was lost.

4.22 On the 21st January 2008 the Acting Governor of Vava'u, Tu'a Taumoepau, acting on the L.9 application that was lodged by Gordon Allison on the 29th June 2007, wrote a Savingram to the Minister of Lands recommending the grant of the lease to Escape Tonga Ltd, the company of Gordon Allison for a term of 20 years (Exhibit 85). Cabinet approved this application on the 26th March 2008 (Exhibit 9) and the lease was registered on the 16th December 2008 (Exhibit 16). The lease application from Nesha Rosic and Island Real Estate Ltd was approved by Cabinet on the 23rd April 2008 (Exhibit 10) for a term of 20 years and registered on the 14th January 2009 (Exhibit 17).

4.23 Relying on the rights that he has been given under the Government approved lease and the "family lease" Gordon Allison has subdivided and constructed a number of buildings on the 3 acre plot of land in Nuapapu Island. He markets these as villas through the internet and so far has sold 8. A copy of the marketing advertisement is attached as Appendix 5 and a copy of one of the agreements is found in Exhibit 98. Nesha Rosic has not constructed any building on his 4 acre leased land yet.

Caveat

4.24 Acting on instructions received from Robert Bryce on behalf of Richard Mortimer, Law Practitioner David Corbett lodged a caveat with the Ministry of Land dated 9th May 2007 to prohibit any dealings with that part of the land which was subject to the Tenancy Agreement because of the "tenancy interest" of Richard Mortimer. Corbett was verbally informed by an officer of the Ministry that the caveat could not be made as the Land Act provides for caveats to be lodged only against leaseholds. No lease had yet been granted in respect of this property.

4.25 A Deed of Lease was granted to the company of Gordon Allison, Escape Tonga Ltd on the 16th December 2008 (Exhibit 16). This was over a 3 acres area that included the 2 acres over which Richard Mortimer had his prior Tenancy Agreement. On the 14th January 2009 another Deed of Lease was registered by the company of Nesha Rosic, Island Real Estate Ltd (Exhibit 17) over the remaining 4 acres that included the 2 acres over which Eric Stark had his prior Tenancy Agreement.34

4.26 On the 23rd June 2009 David Corbett lodged a caveat on behalf of Richard Mortimer (Exhibit 1 Tab AH) and Eric Stark (Exhibit 1 Tab AN) in respect of their interests in their 2 acres that were included in the leases of Escape Tonga Ltd and Island Real Estate Ltd. On the 9th October 2009 Corbett lodged another caveat on behalf of Mortimer over the same 2 acres lot (Exhibit 20).

4.27 In spite of the caveats lodged by David Corbett, construction work on the land concerned have been continued by Gordon Allison who has subdivided the 3 acres lot and advertised and sold these with Villas to foreigners.

4.28 The Commission has been informed by the Secretary of the Ministry of Lands that once the caveat has been registered they stop all dealings and applications in connection with the land, but they have no control over buildings or works or structures on the land. This is covered in the next section.

Building Permit

4.29 On the 7th October 2008, Siaosi Moala who was in charge of the Building Control Division of the Ministry of Works dealing with the issuance of permits for new buildings under the Buildings Act 2002 wrote to Gordon Allison advising him that he did not have a permit to build houses on Nuapapu and to cease such activities until a permit is issued (Exhibits 348 and 348A). In his evidence, Ringo Fa'oliu who is now in charge of this division said that Gordon Allison still does not have a building permit as referred to by Siaosi Moala. When told that in spite of this, Gordon Allison has been and still is constructing buildings without a building licence, Ringo undertook to look into this matter and may require police help to prevent this unlawful activity. When re-called a few days later, Ringo said that he had communicated with Gordon Allison who asked that he be given the opportunity to complete the 8th villa before taking up the permit issue again with the Ministry of Works.

Findings on the Nuapapu Island land deals

4.30 From the facts as related above on the Tenancy Agreements made by Mortimer and Stark in 2006 and the lease Agreements made by Allison and Rosic over the same allotment in Nuapapu Island in 2007 it is very apparent that the situation is in a mess. To complicate matters, Allison has built and sold some of these buildings to foreign clients for substantial money.

4.31 Mortimer and Stark have given substantial amounts of money to the Moleni family in pursuance of the Tenancy Agreements. Allison and Rosic have also given substantial amounts of money to the Moleni family in pursuance of their Lease Agreements.

4.32 The Moleni family knew they had a prior agreement made in 2006 over the land and received substantial money in respect of that agreement but still entered into another agreement in 2007 over the same land and received money in respect of that agreement.

4.33 The justification for the second agreement as claimed by the Moleni family with the support of Rosic and Allison is that there was a default in the payments by Mortimer and Stark which resulted in the termination of their Tenancy Agreements. This was supported by their Lawyer Samiu Vaipulu as seen from his email in Exhibit 106.

4.34 As seen from the evidence, Mortimer and Stark had paid all that were due under their Tenancy Agreements and some monthly rental payments in advance. Rosic and Allison were aware of the Tenancy Agreements but pursued their own Lease Agreements with the Moleni family on the basis that the Tenancy Agreements had lapsed for default in payments and that in any case they were unlawful and therefore void and not registered in the Land Registry.

4.35 The validity of the Tenancy Agreement is based on it not being an agreement over land but an agreement over the use of buildings that are owned by the landowner. They are purely commercial agreements governed by the laws of contract and not subject to the Land Laws of Tonga.

4.36 It is clear that the Moleni family have received substantial money from two sources over the same land. At the end of the day after the mess over these deals are resolved, the Moleni family must be responsible for refunding the money of the party that does not end up with the use of the land. This situation can only be resolved through a decision of the court and we urge the parties to take their dispute to the court for a final resolution.

4.37 The involvement of Government through the Acting Governor and his officers in these land deals will be made part of the court proceedings. The involvement of Government in the Real Estate business and the moratorium placed by the Minister of Labour Commerce and Industries in March 2007 on the issuance of Real Estate Agency Licences will also be part of such court proceedings. We suggest that Government should on its own accord make its own internal inquiry of the involvement of its officers in the Tenancy Agreement and the Lease Agreement over Houmatoka with a view to appropriate disciplinary actions.

4.38 The involvement of the Ministry of Works with regard to the permit for the buildings constructed by Gordon Allison need to be rectified.

CHAPTER 5 – WRITTEN SUBMISSIONS

5.1 In response to the public notices we received letters and submissions mainly from people mostly residing overseas complaining about land deal experiences they had through real estate agents in Vava'u. Richard Mortimer and Eric Stark came from Hong Kong to give evidence in person. Some who resided in Tonga also gave evidence. All letters and submissions were considered by the Commission and appropriate responses were directed to be made by the Secretary.

5.2 It is not the function of the Commission to solve the problems indicated in the submissions. Our function is to investigate the land practices involved and report to His Majesty and Privy Council with recommendations. The aggrieved parties have their proper avenue to seek redress which is ultimately through the Courts of law. Richard Mortimer and Eric Stark (Hong Kong).

5.3 The submissions of Richard Mortimer are found in Exhibits 1, 2, 3 and 4. The submissions of Eric Stark are found in Exhibits 22, 25, 26 and 27.

5.4 The land deal involving Mortimer and Stark revolve around Nuapapu Island and in particular the allotment called Houmatoka owned by the Fe'aomoeata family. This has been fully discussed in Chapter 4 and need not be gone into further detail here. We will refer to the problem posed by the double deal in this allotment in our recommendations at the end of this report. Suffice for us to say that if the parties are not able to settle their dispute, the only solution would be through a properly instigated legal action through the Court.

Paul Kenneth Dickinson (United Kingdom) (Appendix 9)

5.5 Mr. Dickinson is a resident of the United Kingdom. He saw in 2008 a property advertised in the website www.investintonga.com and was interested. The property was in the island of Fofoa in Vava'u and the website belonged to Trevor Jefferson. The total land area is about 16.5 acres and for a term of 80 years. Total cost was US$145,000 plus US$99 per month rent.

5.6 The deal was brokered by Trevor Jefferson by means of a loan to Paul Dickinson of the agreed purchase price of US$145,000 (Exhibit 229). This meant that Jefferson would pay the purchase price to the landowner and Dickinson would repay with monthly instalments of 2000 pounds sterling to Jefferson.

5.7 In pursuance of the loan agreement, Dickinson paid a total of 10,000 pounds sterling. In April 2009 Mr. Dickinson came to Vava'u and met Trevor Jefferson. He did not see the property, but for a number of reasons, including finding out that Jefferson paid only between US$75,000 and US$100,000 to the landowner, he wished to withdraw from the deal and asked for the return of his money on the 4th May 2009. Mr. Jefferson refused saying that Dickinson was suffering from a "buyer's remorse" but as a gesture of goodwill he offered US$9,100 to Dickinson. This would be about US$5000 short of the 10,000 pounds sterling paid by Dickinson. This offer was not accepted by Mr. Dickinson as he wants the whole of the money paid i.e. 10,000 pounds sterling. We feel that this is a matter which Mr. Dickinson can solve only through a private court action.

Alistair and Lesley Allan (Scotland) (Appendix 10)

5.8 This Scottish couple became interested in a property advertised in the www.investintonga.com website of Trevor Jefferson in 2008. The property was Oceanview in Neiafu, Vava'u and consisted of 3/2 homes with 2 stylish rental apartments. The asking price was US$78,700 with a term of 7 years lease which was negotiable. A 10% deposit was required to hold the property.

5.9 Mr. & Mrs. Allan paid the deposit of US$7,870 plus US$250 as escrow fee. The escrow account was held by Hans Schmeiser, the owner of the property. They came to Vava'u in October 2008, felt that there was something wrong with the deal and decided not to go through with it. They asked for the return of their deposit. After some hassle with both Jefferson and Schmeiser, the deposit was returned to Mr. & Mrs. Allan.

5.10 In a letter to their fellow countryman Lord Dalgety, received on the 8th December 2009 it is interesting to note the following comments from Mr. & Mrs. Allan: "We feel that Mr. Jefferson and other ex-patriates are ruining the real estate market in Tonga and cannot understand why these nefarious practices are allowed to continue, but are astonished to see that if you go into the www.investintonga.com website that the entire waterfront in Vava'u appears to be for lease/sale and hope that no one else falls into the same trap as ourselves."

5.11 Mr. Jefferson gave us a different version of what happened (Exhibit 213) indicating that the deposit of US$7,870 paid into the Island Escrow account was not refundable if the buyer does not go through with the purchase. This is shown in the receipt that is part of Exhibit 213. He ends his letter to us under cover dated 18 March 2010 (Exhibit 213) by saying- "I am actually quite shocked they would have anything against me, as stated above, Hans gave them full refund of their deposit even though they did not deserve it, and I never received one seniti of the deposit."

Tim Ellis and Teresa James (United Kingdom) (Appendix 11)

5.12 This English couple was attracted in 2005 to a property in the village of Otea, Kapa Island, Vava'u that was advertised in the website of Robert Bryce. They signed a tenancy agreement (Exhibit 136) with the owners of the land Siokivaha and Lata Vailea on 30 August 2005 for a term of 80 years and paid the sum of US$38,500 plus a monthly rent of US$125.

5.13 At the request of the land owners an amendment was made to the tenancy agreement on the 10th April 2006 (Exhibit 139) whereby the monthly rent was paid 10 years in advance. Again at the request of the Land owners additional voluntary payments were made under an agreement dated 3 April 2008 (Exhibit 141).

5.14 Siokivaha Vailea died in 2008. In October 2009 Tim Ellis and Teresa James were visited by Four Hundred Vailea, a brother of Siokivaha, who claimed that he was the rightful owner of the land.

5.15 Teresa James gave evidence on the 15th March 2010 and confirmed everything said in their letter dated 4 February 2010 to our Secretary (Exhibit 138). In that letter they end with the following: "We like Vava'u and intend to stay here but have decided we would like to sell the resort and run a smaller less demanding business here. In our agreement with Lata and Siokivaha Vailea we made provision for a bonus to be paid to them if we sold the premises, and we will happily extend this to Four Hundred but in order for us to do this we would ask your help in obtaining the correct land agreement document."

5.16 When giving evidence Teresa James tendered the Deed of Grant for this allotment (Exhibit 143). This clearly shows that the owner of the property is Siokivaha Vailea.

5.17 The help requested is "in obtaining the correct land agreement document". The key document here is the Tenancy Agreement dated 30th August 2005 (Exhibit 136) of buildings on part of a tax allotment for 80 years. Like other tenancy agreements mentioned in this report there is a question over the validity of such agreements which has not been brought to the court for a decision.

Mr. Jon Arnott (Tonga) (Appendix 12)

5.18 Mr. Arnott married a Tongan lady, 'Ofa, in 2001 and they have been living in Toula, Vava'u since. In July 2002 'Ofa's parents were offered a piece of land near their home in Toula by 'Ioane Vaha'i for TOP$5000. The understanding was that the allotment would be surrendered to Government and then registered by 'Ofa's brother. The TOP$5000 was paid to 'Ioane and Mr. Arnott and 'Ofa started building on the land.

5.19 In 2003 the adjoining piece of land was offered by 'Ioane for TOP$7000 and the initial payment of TOP$5000 was made (Exhibit 145).

5.20 The land was at the time still held by the mother of 'Ioane as the widow who lived in New Zealand. 'Ioane was acting on his mother's behalf and had kept his mother informed on the land deals.

5.21 Subsequently, a subdivision of the whole tax allotment was made with the help of Robert Bryce for marketing. It became evident to 'Ioane that the land was being offered for a greater price than what he agreed to with Jon Arnott. Through his lawyer he demanded rent of TOP$15,000 per year for each allotment in a letter dated 7 January 2008 (Exhibit 149) for the past two years totaling TOP$60,000. The basis for this demand was that the first agreement was with the widow (his mother) but this ended when the allotment was transferred to 'Ioane in 2005. 'Ioane also stated in evidenced that the payments made by Mr. Arnott were only gifts and not in relation to any agreement.

5.22 The lawyer for Jon Arnott responded pointing to the original agreements for which money was paid and if 'Ioane insisted on taking the land, then he would have to pay for all the buildings and improvements made by Jon Arnott plus the money he paid in pursuance of the agreement totaling about TOP$450,000.41

5.23 'Ofa Arnott gave evidence at the Inquiry. She confirmed the agreements for the two allotments and the payments of the agreed amounts of TOP$5000 and TOP$7000 respectively for each. She also confirmed their understanding that the land would be surrendered to Government to allow her brother to make application for registration.

5.24 'Ioane Vaha'i also gave evidence at the Inquiry. He said that the agreement with his mother as widow ended when he succeeded to the land in 2005. He demanded the lease payments stated in the letter from his lawyer (Exhibit 149) of TOP$15,000 per lot per year from 2005.

5.25 As stated by Jon Arnott in his covering letter dated 28 January 2010 to our Secretary- "It should have been a simple case of surrendering land to the government in our favour. Unfortunately one of the land agents here got involved and 8 years later it still hasn't been resolved".

5.26 This is obviously a matter that can only be resolved through a court action.

Paul and Brenda Burgoon (Canada) (Appendix 13)

5.27 This Canadian couple had an agreement with Hans Schmeiser to take over his company Island Explorer Ltd and the lease agreement with Obey Samate of a property in Neiafutahi. The lease agreement dated 19th April 2006 was for 10 years from 2004 with an option to renew for another 5 years. The rent was TOP$600 per month.

5.28 It would appear that the concern is in the use of the word "rent" as opposed to "lease" because if the landowner, Obey Samate has a mortgage over his land then there cannot be a lease of that land without the approval of the mortgagee.

5.29 The letter to our Secretary dated 15 January 2010 (Exhibit 158) ended by saying- "If we have been defrauded in any way, we would like the commission to help us seek some of our money back from Otto Hans Schmeiser."

5.30 This is another case where the remedy lies with the court.

Sailosi Hemaloto (Tonga) (Appendix 14)

5.31 Sailosi Hemaloto looked after the town allotment of his brother Paula Hemaloto in 'Utungake, Vava'u (Exhibit 167). Paula resided in New Zealand.

5.32 In July 2006 Sailosi was approached by Richard Prestage of New Zealand with a request to lease part of the town allotment. Sailosi informed his brother Paula who agreed to rent the property. A Tenancy Agreement dated 21 August 2006 was signed by the landowner, Hala'api'api Tuituiohu Hemaloto (Paula) and Richard Prestage and his wife Maree for a term of 30 years for a total rent of TOP$20,000 with a right of renewal for a further 30 years at a monthly rental to be agreed (Exhibit 166).

5.33 Sailosi wrote to our Secretary (Exhibit 165) and gave evidence at the Inquiry hearing. He said that he wanted to renegotiate the agreement because the tenant has carried on business activities and given use of the property to another person. Sailosi also said that he had an agreement with the tenant to look after the property while they were out of the country for which he would be paid TOP$50 per month. He entered the property to carry out his caretaking duties and was sued by the occupier for trespass. He was found guilty and ordered not to enter the property again.

5.34 The tenancy Agreement (Exhibit 166) clearly state that the premises may be used for residential and/or commercial purposes in connection with tourism. The agreement also allows subletting and assignment. So it would appear that

Sailosi will be fighting an uphill battle should he wish to renegotiate the agreement.

5.35 This is however, another case where the remedy lies with the court should the parties wish to pursue such.

Felisiano Tolati Fifita (Tonga) (Appendix 15)

5.36 Felisiano Fifita held a tax allotment in Fofoa Island, Vava'u. He wrote to our Secretary on the 14th January 2009 complaining about a land deal he made with Hans Schmeiser (Exhibit 55).

5.37 In 2005 a part of the allotment was given to Olle Ottebu of Zambia under a Tenancy Agreement dated 26 August 2005 (Exhibit 204). The agreement was for a term of 50 years for the payment of US$35,000 plus a monthly rent of US$120. Felisiano says that he received the upfront payment totaling US$25,030 plus US$720 representing 6 month 43 rent in advance on the 6th September 2005. US$10,000 would have been taken by Schmeiser as his commission and expenses in line with the Aleapau Ngaue dated 2 November 2005 with Felisiano (Exhibit 202).

5.38 Schmeiser approached Felisiano again requesting the remaining 4 acres for marketing for a term of 50 years for the payment of TOP$30,000 plus a monthly rent of TOP$120. Payment was made in accordance with an offer and acceptance by Feliciano dated 20th March 2006 (Exhibit 53). The payment was to be made in 3 instalments of TOP$9000 each on 6 March 2006, 9 June 2006 and 9 August 2006 making a total of TOP$27,000.

5.39 He also says that he has not received any of rent of TOP$120 per month. He now wants Schmeiser to vacate his land and seeks the help of the Commission.

5.40 The request for help is outside our terms of reference and Felisiano needs to seek satisfaction through other means possibly through a court action.

Dana Stephenson (Tonga) (Appendix 16)

5.41 Ms Dana Stephenson, Law Practitioner, wrote to our Secretary on the 1st February 2010 in response to the public notice for information in relation to possible unlawful land dealings in Vava'u (Exhibit 56A). She referred us to three cases where clients had contacted her for advice. These were in relation to properties in Olo'ua Island, Vaka'eitu Island and Nuapapu Island all in Vava'u. All dealings were made by Nesha Rosic.

5.42 Ms Stephenson advised her clients that Nesha Rosic did not have a real estate licence (Olo'ua Island) thus persuading the client to deal directly with the landowner; the lease agreement (Vaka'eitu Island) "was invalid and of no legal effect on the basis that it appeared to be a sale of a tax allotment in excess of the 20 year term allowed by law" and that "it was my opinion that Nesha Rosic was trying to get a quick commission out of my client for a lease application that clearly could not, in terms of the law, be approved by Cabinet"; the lease agreement (Nuapapu Island) "provided was contrary to law and that they would not receive a separate and indefeasible registerable lease for the property as had been explained to them they would in consideration of the AUD$170,000 they were being asked to pay" by Nesha Rosic and Gordon Allison.

5.43 Ms Stephenson found that the Nuapapu Island deal was advertised in the Bayleys Real Estate circular in New Zealand. She accordingly lodged a formal complaint with the Real Estate Agents Authority in December 2009 (Exhibit 56G). The decision of the Authority 44 made on the 23rd March 2010 is in Exhibit 371. Ms Stephenson does not agree with the decision but does not think it worthwhile appealing.

5.44 Ms Stephenson gave some useful suggestions regarding matters that should be
considered and conditions before a real estate licence is issued (Exhibit 373). She has also drawn the attention of the authorities to the unlawful practice of real estate agents in drafting legal documents (Exhibit 374).

Trevor Jefferson (Vava'u) (Appendix 17)

5.45 Trevor Jefferson gave a written report to the Commission dated 13 March 2010 (Exhibit 224) on Tongan Real Estate Problems, Plans and Solutions. The Commission wishes to thank him for taking time to make this report. It has some good suggestions which the Commission will take into consideration in making its recommendations.

CHAPTER 6 – CLOSING REMARKS

6.1 This phase of our work involved the investigation into the possible unlawful dealing with land through the internet. Primarily this concerned land deals in Vava'u which we have referred to in detail in the previous chapters.

6.2 It is always difficult to deal with any contract through the internet. Advertisements are made through the internet may not reflect the true situation here in Tonga. This is more so where transaction with land is concerned where Tongan land law is unusual in the sense that it does not have freehold titles and the internationally recognized concept of sale of land is forbidden by law. Leaseholds are allowed but they have certain restrictions depending on the type of holding involved.

6.3 The Commission has observed real estate agents trying to get around the strict requirements of Tongan land law with long term tenancy agreements over buildings on the land and those to be constructed. The real estate agents say that these are private contracts between the parties that do not affect the ownership of the land and buildings. That the land and buildings are retained and owned by the landowner and therefore the contract is not bound by the Tongan Land Act and is not restricted nor need to go through the process required by that Act.

6.4 The Commission have also observed other real estate Agents using a long term lease agreement with the family (land owner, wife (widow rights) and heir) with the understanding that this binds the family even though such are not allowed by law in respect of land that are held as tax allotments with which most of the Vava'u land deals were involved.

6.5 There is no law or procedure for the registration of Tenancy Agreements in Tonga. So a search of the Lands Office and its Registry will not show whether a particular piece of land is subject to a tenancy agreement over the building on the land. The only person who would know this important land interest is the landowner and the tenant.

6.6 The biggest problem the Commission encountered was the land deal in respect of the property Houmatoka in the island of Nuapapu. This has been fully discussed in the previous chapters and the Commission suggestion is that the problem can only be solved through a properly conducted court action. Legislation by the Legislative Assembly may remedy and clarify the legal standing of such future agreements, but any new legislation cannot be retrospective (under the Tongan Constitution) hence the requirement for court action in the Houmatoka issue. Therefore, in the absence of any clear law on these points, a final court decision will have to be made on the agreement made, the legality of the Tenancy Agreement, the legality of the subsequent lease agreement and the lease granted by Government and the large amount of money received by the landowner. It is not the Commission's function to give a decision or an opinion on this matter. It is best left for the jurisdiction of the court.

6.7 The possible unlawful land dealings in Vava'u revolve around the agreements that grant a greater term of years than that allowed by law. By law, a tax allotment can be leased for only 20 years plus an option for another 10 years. The validity of the tenancy agreement or a lease agreement for 50 to 99 years will determine whether these were unlawful dealings in land.

6.8 The Commission wishes to thank all those who took time to write in with their views and submissions. The Commission also want to thank also all those who were summonsed and gave evidence at our Inquiry. The Commission's work and report is subject to our terms of reference. Our Inquiry has revealed many matters that need to be resolved. In all cases, if the matters cannot be settled amicably, then we suggest that the proper avenue is through the court system and further clarifying legislation.

CHAPTER 7 – RECOMMENDATIONS

7.1 Following our inquiry into possible unlawful land dealings through the internet, the Royal Land Commission makes the following recommendations:

a) That legislation is enacted on a priority basis for the clarification, registration and control of all Tenancy Agreements;

b) That the majority of the existing land related matters considered by the Commission can be processed with in court to determine their legal standing. In doing so, the lawfulness of a range of long term Tenancy Agreements discussed herein, can be finally and properly determined by the court;

c) That greater control is placed on the issuance of a Real Estate License and that greater restrictions and qualification requirements be put in place regarding academic qualification, experience, credit ratings and financial viability;

d) That a National Real Estate Authority be established to govern, control and discipline those carrying on the business of real estate agents;

e) That the National Real Estate Authority monitors, control and discipline the use of the internet for land deals by Real Estate Agents licensed in Tonga;

f) Part of the work of the National Real Estate Authority is to ensure that Real Estate Agents are not involved in unlawful dealing with land and do not give legal advice to clients or landowners if they are not licensed to practice law in Tonga;

g) That there is an ongoing and timely cooperation between the National Real Estate Authority and the Ministry of Lands in the exchange of information in order to make available to the public any agreement that involves a particular allotment of land;

h) That Government investigate the whole background to the registration of the name of Piea Fe'aomoeata in the Land Registration Book in relation to the property Houmatoka in Nuapapu Island, Vava'u on the 29th June 2007, when his father who was registered as owner in the Deed of Grant was still alive, and the involvement of the then Acting Governor Tu'a Taumoepeau and the land registration officer 48 Makafilia Mafi including their involvement and approval of the L9 application for lease on the same day by Escape Vava'u Ltd and Island Real Estate Ltd;

i) That the Ministry of Labour, Commerce and Industries explain and justify the moratorium placed by the Minister on the issuance of Real Estate Licences in Tonga from March 2007 and why Vava'u has been treated differently from Tongatapu;

j) That the Ministry of Works follows up and explain why it has allowed the construction of buildings in Nuapapu Island by Gordon Allison to continue without a building permit as required by law;
k) That consideration be given to increasing the existing number of years that a tax
allotment may be leased;
l) That the Ministry of Lands' duties regarding the registration and enforcement of caveats be strengthened and put into effect;
m) That the above recommendations are pursued in conjunction with the Commission's recommendations in its Interim Phase One Report to improve the overall efficiency and performance of the Ministry of Land.

JATROPHA - BIOLOGICAL DETAILS

Jatropha flowering plant in the spurge family, Euphorbiaceae. The name is derived from the Greek words for physician and nutrition, hence Jatropha's common name physic-nut.There are approximately 170 species, mostly native to the Americas (although 66 species are found in the Old World) and some like the plant we were interested in, Jatropha Curcas, are deciduous. As with many members of the family Euphorbiaceae, *Jatropha* contains compounds that are highly toxic.

In 2007, Jatropha Curcas was identified by Goldman Sachs as one of the best candidates for future biodiesel production because is drought and pest resistant and produces seeds containing 27-40%oil. The remaining press cake of Jatropha seeds after oil extraction could also be considered for energy production. The only down sides are that Jatropha contains some toxic compounds and none of the species have been properly domesticated and so productivity is variable, and the long-term impact of their large-scale use on soil quality and the environment is unknown.

Where already grown the oil from Jatropha Curcas is mainly converted into biodiesel for use in diesel engines. The cake can be used for fish or animal feed (if detoxified), biomass feedstock to power electricity plants, or as biogas or high-quality organic fertilizer. It can also be used as a bio-pesticide and for medicinal purposes.

Furthermore, it has been found that Jatropha Curcas can be planted in arid and hot regions and contribute a reduction of up to 25 t of CO_2 per hectare per year from the atmosphere (over a 20 yr period), while still producing bio fuel and also the dry cakes from the oil extraction. Currently, research plantations are being planted to test the results and test future economic viability.

The seeds of Jatropha Curcas contain the highly poisonous toxalbumin curcin as well as carcinogenic phorbol. Despite this, the seeds are occasionally eaten after roasting, which reduces some of the toxicity. Its sap is a skin irritant, and ingesting as few as three untreated seeds can be fatal to humans.

Obviously a plant to be handled with care which presumably explains why in Tonga the fruiting elements of Jatropha are removed as part of its long-standing use as a shade plant for the vanilla crop.

SELECTED NON-FICTION FROM APS BOOKS
(www.andrewsparke.com)

Aramoana (Andrew Sparke)
Bella In The Wych-Elm (Andrew Sparke)
Croc Curry & Texas Tea: Surviving Nigeria (Paul Dickinson)
Istanbul: The Visitor Essentials (Andrew Sparke)
More Swings Than Roundabouts (John Wright)
Piggery Jokery In Tonga (Andrew Sparke)
Rear Gunner (Andrew Sparke)
Stutthof (Andrew Sparke)
The Devil's Cauldron (Pete Merrill)
The Strange Free-Fall Of Fred Ryland (Helen Pitt)
The Ways Of Mevagissey (Andrew Sparke)
War Shadows (Andrew Sparke)
What I Think About When I Think about Aikido (Mark Peckett)
Who Put Bella In The Wych Elm? Vol.1 The Crime Scene Revisited (Alex Merrill)

www.ingramcontent.com/pod-product-compliance
Ingram Content Group UK Ltd.
Pitfield, Milton Keynes, MK11 3LW, UK
UKHW021924190726
13853UKWH00002B/835

9 798201 931445